35⁰

Painting in England
1500–1870

PAINTING
IN ENGLAND
1500–1870
by
David Piper

THE BOOK SOCIETY

LONDON

Privately published by The Book Society
6 Baker Street, London

▪▪▪▪▪▪▪▪▪▪▪▪▪▪▪▪▪▪▪▪▪▪▪▪▪▪▪▪▪▪

The medallion portrait on the binding
is based (in reverse) on an
unpublished drawing of J. M. W. Turner
by C. R. Leslie; reproduced
by courtesy of A. L. Gordon Esq.

INSIDE FRONT AND BACK COVERS
"STONEHENGE" BY JOHN CONSTABLE

Contents

Illustrations

The publishers wish to express their gratitude to all galleries and private collectors who have kindly given permission for their paintings to be reproduced in this volume

The endpapers are from John Constable's *Drawing of Stonehenge* (15″ × 23¹/₂″)
in the Victoria and Albert Museum, London.

THE 16TH AND 17TH CENTURIES

The luxury of having non-utilitarian furniture about the house was acclimatized only relatively late in England—furniture that is not for sitting on or for storing things in, but purely ornamental. Painted pictures are one kind of such ornament, wall-furniture; we are so accustomed to them now, that a wall can look bare without them, but it was not always so. In the Middle Ages, painting was hardly ever conceived in order simply to give pleasure; it was functional and educative, and its subjects were normally not of the here but of the hereafter. On the walls of churches, the frescoes unrolled the Bible stories and in the breviaries the brilliant miniatures were so to speak aids to gracious praying. Only in the Renaissance did the art of painting begin to specialize in more avowedly aesthetic pleasure, contracting off the church walls and the altars into easel paintings, and setting up a portable world of its own within the gold frame. Its subjects too become more mundane, and concentrate on man in his earthly setting; a revival of interest in presenting an illusion, both of man in all the pride of flesh and life and of the three-dimensional world in which he lived, precipitated the re-discovery of the necessary techniques of best achieving that illusion—the artifice of perspective, known to the Greeks and the Romans, but abandoned (doubtless as irrelevant to their purposes) by the Middle Ages. The technique of painting in oil was developed, permitting a much greater brilliance and subtlety in colour and modelling. These techniques were first exploited fully in the Netherlands by painters like the Van Eycks, and in Italy; by 1500, the three giants of the High Renaissance were already at the beginning or in the middle of their careers—Leonardo da Vinci, Raphael and Michelangelo.

But about that time England was, in matters of material civilization as of geography, on the fringe of Europe. Except for rare moments in history, she has always tended in matters of art, not to initiate, but to tag along some way behind. But it is also very difficult to formulate any valid judgement of what painting was going on in England at this time, because so much of it was subsequently deliberately destroyed by the Puritans. What is left suggests that a somewhat out-of-date imitation of Netherlandish painting was fashionable, but it is also clear that the English aristocracy had not yet acquired the habit of decorating the walls and cabinets of great private houses with paintings. Apart from religious

HANS HOLBEIN *Lady with Squirrel* c. 1527

paintings, such pictures as there were, were functional, and they were probably mainly portraits. The first English king of whom there remains any considerable number of portraits is Henry VII; he was concerned, after the Battle of Bosworth in 1485, to stamp his image on his subjects' minds as that of king in fact, thereby helping to obscure the most questionable problem as to whether he was also king by right. Such paintings had a very specific purpose, as did the pictures of princesses that their fathers, seeking advantageous alliances, sent with details of dowries to the most promising bachelors.

The first full impact of the startling possibilities of Renaissance painting upon English eyes was that of the Swiss-German painter, Hans Holbein, between 1527 and his death in London in 1543. Holbein was one of the greatest artists of the European Renaissance; the especial characteristic of his genius was perhaps his unmatched skill in reconciling the brute facts, down to the minutest detail, of the physical appearance of the world with the rigorous demands of that purely pictorial construction that supports all great works in the Renaissance tradition. But what must have shocked, and delighted, the relatively unsophisticated courtiers of Henry VIII, is the sheer sleight-of-hand magic of the illusion; nothing of this vividness and solidity had been seen in England before. It so happened that Holbein only began to be employed by Henry VIII himself when the English Reformation was well under way. Until then, the Church had been the dominant patron of the arts; now, as all image-making in religion was anathema to Protestants, artists had to seek patronage from the laity. In painting, this patronage demanded above all portraits of itself, and in England the emphasis on portraiture remained constant for the next two hundred years. Painters too have to eat, and this was the only branch of painting that was likely to bring in a steady living. Yet, while the art seemed to have been dealt a heavy blow from the one side, from another it received encouragement; Henry VIII was a European potentate very much of his time, and conscious of European fashions of demonstrating princely magnificence. Paintings had become part of the decor of European monarchy, and Henry VIII's inventories show that he was aware of it. From his example, the fashion slowly spread, and, once rooted, it was to go on spreading ever more widely as the standard of living rose.

We are lucky to have so great an artist as Holbein as the first monument in our modern painting, yet it is curious how isolated he stands. For, in

14   HANS HOLBEIN Detail, from *The Ambassadors* 1533

terms of artistic style and its development in painting, he had surprisingly little influence—there is no real English school developing out of his work. The reason probably lies in the peripheral nature of English art again; Englishmen, out on the fringe, tended not so much to develop on their own, but—in art as in costume—to reach in as it were, into the seething centres of the Continent, and to grab thence the latest styles—and the latest practitioners of those styles. Thus between 1500 and about 1750, the dominant styles in English painting are, with one exception, all imported, and so too the dominant artists tend to be foreigners also.

The first painter of consequence after Holbein was a Fleming who signed his pictures HE (believed to be Hans Eworth), active here between about 1545 and 1573. Already no longer of the High Renaissance, he brought with him the Flemish version of the style that succeeded it—Mannerism; that is, the -ism based on the later manner of Michelangelo's style, a strained, exaggerated style that reacted against the classic balance and poise of Raphael. In Eworth's painting shown here (**p. 49**), dated 1550, all the characteristics of this style are deployed and with fascinating if ultimately unconvincing ingenuity wedded to a very realistic portrait head. As an illusion, although details are fairly naturalistically painted, it does not add up; it is an allegory in picture, and the pictorial values are subordinate to the message. Much of its meaning is now lost, but we know it to represent Sir John Luttrell, soldier and trader (he died at Woolwich, of the sweat, in the year this was painted, when preparing for an expedition to Morocco). The goddess in the clouds appears to be Peace, extending a helping hand (her attendants have already salvaged his money bags, his warhorse and arms, from the storm) but the import is obscure, and various mottoes inscribed about the picture do not enlighten. This sort of portrait does not seem to have caught on with many clients, and in his later portraits Eworth points in style to a uniquely English development of European Mannerism, in the work of the English-born miniaturist Nicholas Hilliard and of the Elizabethan court-painters. In them, a certain emphasis on linear design, rather than on modelling in the round, is evident; the aim seems to be, not so much to catch a sitter's physical likeness, but to demonstrate him almost like a theorem, as a cypher of rank, blood and fashion. This trends reaches a climax in the portraits of Elizabeth herself; she appears as a stiff, quasi-religious image, set up in an airless niche for adoration. On a life-size scale, the method can be very vapid; concentrated to miniature by Hilliard it

produced some lyrical images of an unrivalled jewel-like purity and
brilliance. The miniature reproduced here (p. 50) is far from photograph-
ic, but it is a supremely apt realization of a lovelorn hero, perhaps from
one of Shakespeare's earlier plays—this could be Benedick or Mercutio.
In fact, it may well represent the Earl of Essex, tangled in a symbolic
and thorny rose-thicket of love for his virgin queen, in his golden youth
before ambition went sour on him.

This courtier style flourished till the reign of Charles I, when it was
literally liquidated by the arrival of yet another immigrant style, the
Baroque. Its champion in England was the Fleming, Van Dyck, and it
is in his vision that the romantic, brilliant, and doomed generation of
the Cavaliers still lives. It is as though a window had been opened; a
faint breeze ripples through the picture, everything is in movement;
the silks and lace shimmer in light, and the picture space opens back to
green landscapes, to the shifting sky, along strongly stressed diagonals;
the flesh is iridescent, almost breathing. Like Holbein's, Van Dyck's
genius owed much to his power of marrying a most precise individual
characterisation into a grand pictorial design, but with him the design
is much more open and more sensuous, moving with an easy and supreme-

ly elegant rhetoric. His elegance and his sensuousness enliven even the paint itself; his paint seduces, and it has seduced countless English painters ever since—as Gainsborough said on his death-bed: 'We shall all go to heaven, and Van Dyck is of the company'.

Van Dyck died in 1641; his only English rival of stature, William Dobson, survived him by only five years. Dobson painted the Cavaliers as soldiers, or else—as in his masterpiece here, *Endymion Porter* (p. 51)— as gorgeous, full-blown but entirely credible, even gross, English country gentlemen. Different in mood though he is, Dobson stands generally within the tradition of which Van Dyck was master, and which was to dominate English portraiture for the next hundred years. To Van Dyck the Fleming, succeeded Peter Lely the Dutchman, the dominant painter till his death in 1680, modulating Van Dyck's early morning subtleties into a coarser mode, sonorous in colour, opulent, fleshy in paint (p. 52)— a perfect recorder of the worldly court of Charles II. To him in turn succeeded Sir Godfrey Kneller, a German baronet, commanding painting in England until the seventeen-twenties; a leaner, more astringent talent, generalizing his sitters even further until one may be hard put to it, to

SIR ANTHONY VAN DYCK
(*left*) *Sir Thomas Hanmer* c. 1638 and
(*above*) Detail

SIR GODFREY KNELLER *Viscount Shannon* (unfinished) c. 1710

distinguish one sitter from another; the painter of the high, aloof mask of the Augustan age.

By Kneller's time, portraiture had developed along almost mass-production lines; the demand had become so great that some such solution was forced upon the most fashionable painters. The master himself, while in control of the overall design, painted perhaps no more than the head; the rest was done by assistants. The unfinished head shown here is as much perhaps as Kneller painted himself of many of his portraits, but it also shows the individual brilliance of his hand. With his successors, the practice became even more mechanical, and about twelve of London's leading painters all relied on one expert (Joseph van Aken) to paint the draperies in their portraits. Inevitably, the finished product lost in vitality and freshness, and became stiff, monotonous, and deadly formal (p. 44).

By now, other branches of painting were flourishing in England—landscape, subject paintings of historical or mythological scenes, still-life, genre, sea-pieces and so on. A gentleman's standards of furnishing now demanded pictures of all kinds; a considerable proportion of these were imported, and more were produced here by immigrant artists mostly only of secondary rank, mainly Netherlanders but also some French and Italian; the styles in which they worked were also imported. Exceptional, in quality, were the Dutch Van de Veldes, father and son, in the reigns of the later Stuarts; they are the source of the brilliant school of English Marine painters. But, by the second quarter of the eighteenth century, there are at last signs of a true, original and native outbreak of painting in England.

WILLEM VAN DE VELDE, THE YOUNGER *Drawing* 1700

WILLEM VAN DE VELDE, THE ELDER *Drawing* 1681

HOGARTH

Hogarth used to be called the Father of English Painting, but it is a label that is only true if you take it to mean that he was the first in time of the great English-born painters of the eighteenth century. Though history in its deepening perspective has now revealed him, in the full European context, as the most important English painter of the century, the calibre of his greatness was far from recognized by his contemporaries in this country, and he had no artistic progeny here, no followers of any consequence to carry on and develop his style. In fact he spent his life in conflict with the fashionable taste of his time, embattled against the connoisseurs—a bitter struggle for any artist to undertake, for it was the connoisseurs who controlled, as far as painting was concerned, the artist's livelihood, by what they bought or did not buy.

The scale of values by which the eighteenth century assessed works of art was the natural and logical outcome of a classical and Mediterranean education. In literature, the highest possible form was held to be the grand epic, challenging comparison with Homer and with Virgil; so too, in painting, a truly major work could be nothing less than the visual equivalent of the epic, the history painting: the representation of some heroic scene from classical history or mythology. Only in this sort of art, it was felt, could the abilities of the artist be most fully extended, and the highest faculties of the spectator most meaningfully exercised. All other kinds of painting were, in comparison with history-painting, only minor ventures; painting, wrote the connoisseur John Elsum in 1703, 'is like Musick, best in Concert. History-Painting is that Concert, comprizing all the other Parts of Painting, and the principal end of it is to move the Passions'. Any painter ambitious of greatness had therefore to answer this challenge, and the history of English painting for over a hundred years is strewn with their failures, interesting as corpses for academic dissection, impotent as corpses 'to move the Passions' of the modern onlooker. Yet the problem, for the painters who strove with it, was far from academic; with it was bound up the whole question of the honour of their art. At the beginning of the eighteenth century, the professional status of a painter was still uneasy; the Elizabethan Stow had stigmatized painting as 'base and mechanical, and a mere mestier of an Artificer and handy Craftsman', certainly no career for a gentleman, and much

theoretical writing about painting after that was concerned with the rehabilitation, intellectually and socially, of the artist. This explains Jonathan Richardson's pleasure when he was able to establish (to his own satisfaction at least) that Raphael was superior to Virgil, the argument being that the painter (of histories) had to have the same knowledge of art, science and histories as did the writer, plus one talent that the writer did not have, that of the 'Curious Artificer'. Richardson wrote early in the century; his theories were vindicated by the career, writings, and to an extent, the practice, of Sir Joshua Reynolds—the pictures by which Reynolds succeeded were not strictly 'history-pictures'. And although artists were to be recognized as it were as worthy and fully-fledged members of society at last, the stickiness of the market in which they had to sell their most ambitious wares is best illustrated by the story of the patron who went to view Benjamin West's painting of *Pylades and Orestes*, yet did not buy it even though he liked it. Upon his son querying his decision against it, he said: 'You surely would not have me hang a modern English picture in my house, unless it were a portrait?' For the rich English patron, his education polished off by the Grand Tour, great Art was a monopoly of the Continent, and mainly of Italy.

The snobbery and quackery that this attitude could breed only too easily were a constant butt of Hogarth's satire; Hogarth's nationalistic fervour could indeed come close to chauvinism. Reynolds, in a self-portrait we shall consider later, is accompanied by a bust of Michelangelo; in Hogarth's self-portrait, the artist is accompanied into posterity by his dog, his palette (the tools of the trade, not mentioned in Reynolds' portrait), and by the works of Shakespeare, Milton, and—significantly—of Swift. Yet Hogarth himself was not immune to the lure of the history-picture in the continental manner; he was after all the son-in-law of Sir James Thornhill, the best English master of huge Baroque decor, whose exertions can be seen on the walls and ceiling of the great Painted Hall at Greenwich. Hogarth regarded himself as, amongst other things, the heir to the Grand Manner, and made various attempts in that manner. These are not, in fact, contemptible as contemporaries asserted; yet, while mostly worthy, respectable, and even, historically, of importance, they are boring. His genius was not for such generalized statements in an established tradition, but for a precise and lively comment on particular fact. If his work is uneven in quality throughout his career, its liveliness is never in doubt, served by a quick and deft command of his paint in which the heavy undulations of the Baroque break into the run and flicker of the Rococo. He loathed symmetry (beloved of contemporary neo-classic connoisseurs of the school of the Earl of Burlington), and put his faith in the 'beauty of a composed intricacy of form' that 'leads the eye a kind of chase', along a serpentine line through three dimensions —his famous S-line, the theory of which he developed in his book, *The Analysis of Beauty*. All his best work invites the eye to this kind of dance. It is there even in his straightforward head-and-shoulders portraits— which offer also a veracity and plainness new to English portraiture, if not generally a very searching characterization; it is there likewise in various degree in his earliest efforts at conversation-pieces, small-scale family groups, made in the seventeen thirties, and especially it enlivens his series of pictorial satires.

The first of these famous series was *The Harlot's Progress* of 1731 (the originals were burnt in 1755), and the second, *The Rake's Progress*, finished by 1735 and now in Sir John Soane's Museum. Hogarth seems to have hit on the idea of these series by accident, but once conceived, it was soon backed by a deliberate programme, the claims of which were stressed by his friend and sympathizer, the novelist Henry Fielding. The writer saw in Hogarth a great comic history painter, even as he held himself to be a serious comic epic prose writer. 'The Epic, as well as the Drama', wrote Fielding, 'is divided into Tragedy and Comedy'; the two are of equal intellectual stature. Hogarth's satires were not burlesques; besides being, in the formal sense, serious painting, they were also serious moral and social satires. He was entirely in key, if not with the patrons of high art, then with the moral and philanthropic mood of his age, as expressed in the life and work of such men as the Fieldings, Henry and his brother John, one of the first of the great Metropolitan magistrates. His art was, in the modern term, 'committed': a reflection, an interpretation and a commentary on the social condition of his time. He found inspiration, not in other people's art (though he borrowed readily and without acknowledgement from a great variety of sources), but in life and nature on his doorstep and in the London streets: 'my Picture was my Stage, and men and women my actors, who were by means of certain actions and expressions to exhibit a dumb show'.

The Rake's Progress, like the other series, was made a commercial possibility by its widespread sale in engraved form (the paintings were basically only one stage towards the engravings, which perhaps partly accounts for their unevenness). In the first scene, Tom Rakewell enters unexpectedly, still a student, upon his inheritance. In the second scene, reproduced here (p. 54), we see him at his morning levee as a sort of trainee man of the world, but beset already by money-sucking parasites. The anteroom beyond is full of vendors of personal finery; in the fore-

WILLIAM HOGARTH Detail, from *The Levee* (in colour p. 54) c. 1732

ground the hero is surrounded by the necessary retainers of a young blood. His musician is thumping out the *Rape of the Sabines*; crowded about him are a landscape gardener, a fencing master, quarterstaff instructor, and on the walls behind, evidence that one of those dealers in 'Old Masters' had already found an easy victim in the young man. The vanity and busy vapidness of Tom, still rather gauche, face advancing from brow to nose and retreating swiftly from nose to chin, are succinctly portrayed, and the crowd around sharply individualized (they are said to be all portraits—Dubois, the fencing master, was killed in a duel in 1734). With its parade of futile gesture and almost audible cacophony, the painting demonstrates the squandering of a young man's character before it is even formed. In the next four paintings the tempo speeds up: Tom is seen drunk, in poor shape, being robbed by girls in a brothel.

27

Then he is arrested for debt; the situation is salvaged, by marriage with an aged decrepit heiress, only to be lost again in a gaming house, and thence to the Fleet prison and the last terrible view of Tom, naked and raving, in Bedlam. Such a moral tale was not of course new in literature or even entirely so in painting, but it lives by the brilliance of the painter's observation and improvisation, and by a sort of counterpoint of visual, purely formal elegance against the harsh and often squalid subject matter (this technique was brought to its peak in *The Marriage-à-la-Mode* in the National Gallery).

In his early pictures, his characters sometimes teem in his inventiveness almost to overcrowding, even in his straight conversation-pieces. He abandoned these (they did not pay well for the labour expended) and the *Lord George Graham in his Cabin* (p. 55), painted about 1745 probably in celebration of a successful naval action off Ostend, is a late exercise in a genre he had virtually abandoned. It is however one of his happiest portrait groups, the antithesis of a formal family portrait; even the sloping walls of the ship seem relaxed in easy pleasure. His exuberance is under perfect control; for once he uses an almost symmetrical composition, the figures grouped as on a stage, but surely in deliberate light mockery in honour of the comic opera, with the dogs taking the leading part, that seems to be in progress. The composition has in fact a fresh and haunting lilt and swing that is anchored firmly on the little upright, bewigged figure of the pugdog on the right. The noise—mercifully unheard—would be appalling; the visual rhythm is enchanting.

Five years before this, Hogarth had painted his masterpiece on the life-size scale—'the portrait that I painted with most pleasure, and in which I particularly wished to excel, was that of Captain Coram for the Foundling Hospital' (p. 56). The sitter, a former captain in the Merchant Service, was a key figure in that moral, socially philanthropic movement with which Hogarth was in such sympathy. In 1738, Coram had founded the Foundling Hospital, with which Hogarth was associated in a gesture which was characteristically both genuinely charitable and designed to advertise the arts (and himself). He gave his portrait of Coram to the Hospital, an example followed by other artists; these pictures were open for people to see, and in effect constituted the first public exhibition gallery of pictures in England. Hogarth's faith in his own contribution has been amply justified, and it still stands as one of the most remarkable European portraits of the eighteenth century. Designed as a set-piece

28

WILLIAM HOGARTH Detail, from *The Polling* (in colour p. 57) c. 1754

in the grand manner, a formal portrait for the board room of a charitable
institution, it is based, in composition, on a portrait by the French master
of the court-portrait, Rigaud (a portrait which Hogarth knew by an
engraving of it). But while enough of the conventional rhetoric—the
pillar and drapery, the accumulation of furniture, and the deliberately
self-conscious pose of the figure—have been retained to set the picture
amongst its peers as a formal portrait, the whole conception has been
subtly modulated to convey also the essential informality, the honesty
both forthright and unassuming of the seventy-year old sea-captain.
Bluff, gay, he sits there, a man happy in his duty, his legs scarce long
enough to reach the ground. It is, as it were, an aristocratic platitude
entirely revitalized by its translation, with unerring sensibility, into middle-
class terms. There are countless society portraits almost identical in pose
and accessories, and giving the impression that their sitters are about to
unburden themselves of an opening speech of unbearable tedium. If
Coram were to open his mouth, it would be to comment—as he did
at Dr. Mead's table, on the toast to the Governors of the Foundling
Hospital—hoping 'the new ones will be better than the last, who were
rogues enough'. 'But these Governors,' said the startled Dr Mead: 'You
don't suppose? . . .' 'I expect little better than the former'.

29

In the last decade of his life, a rather battered and certainly embittered figure, Hogarth made one more series—*The Election Entertainment:* four paintings satirizing English electoral procedure and said to be based on the Oxfordshire Election of 1754. In the third picture, *The Polling* (p. 57), the climax is near, and the parties are throwing in their last reserves, even a three-quarters-dead hospital patient being heaved up the steps to the booth to give his vote if at the cost of his last breath. In the background there is an unusually overt and direct criticism: Britannia in person broken down in her coach while her drivers wrangle amongst themselves. Designed, like the other series, for engraving and so needing plenty of incident to sell, this again teems with life and movement, and in its pleasant landscape setting, that looks forward to Rowlandson, offers a new aspect of Hogarth's work.

18TH CENTURY LANDSCAPE

By the time of Hogarth's death in 1764, a new generation had already established itself in London, with a new kind of art and a new attitude to art. The foundation of the Royal Academy in 1769, gave artists, or at least those artists whom it accepted, a social and intellectual Establishment, with a constitution; a school; and an annual mart in which artists' wares could be displayed. It was not of course the first Academy of art in England, but none of the others had had royal patronage and, more important, none of them had lasted, split by the usual internecine jealousies to which artists seem particularly prone. The Royal Academy (though it had no dearth of jealousies) endured, and presently, in his famous *Discourses* delivered annually to the students, its President Sir Joshua Reynolds began to formulate its creed. Reynolds was not only the leading practitioner, but he was, in a way unknown in English society hitherto, profoundly in harmony with the dominant artistic mood of the time and with its whole intellectual and social temper—the metropolitan culture whose centre was London. This however does not prove that he painted greater pictures than some others who stood more or less clear of the Academy mainstream. By 1750, a number of native-born artists were making very fair livings in branches other than the 'safe' one of portrait-painting. It was probably generally difficult to get started in such lines, and evidently impossible to interest certain patrons with continental tastes at all; but nevertheless there were distinguished painters in landscape, sea-painting and animal-painting, quite apart from Hogarth's innovation of satirical comic painting. For Englishmen it may be true that landscape and animal-painting, and to an extent sea-painting, have always been best loved when they retain something of portraiture—are portraits, in fact, recognizable likenesses of their own parks, houses or cities, of their ships or sea-battles. Even the ideal landscapes that they bought abroad were often souvenirs of a golden voyage of youth, echoes of Italy and a classical past—Claude and Gaspar Poussin.

The best landscapes painted in England at the close of the seventeenth and the beginning of the eighteenth centuries were certainly topographical in nature, by artists of Dutch or Flemish origin, and then most notably by Wootton and by George Lambert, a colleague and contemporary of Hogarth who on occasion could give an agreeable flavour of Gaspar Poussin, a touch of romance, to the portraits of his clients' English country houses. In marine-painting, the leading figure was Samuel Scott, also a contemporary of Hogarth, who began by painting in the manner of the Van de Veldes (he owned many drawings by them, and his early pictures often get attributed to them), but who later switched to townscape, almost certainly in answer to a demand that had been created by yet another foreigner—Canaletto. It is tempting to consider Canaletto as an integral part of the English school; it is indeed almost justifiable to do so. His chief clients were almost all English (there are still more Canalettos in this country than anywhere else) and his unofficial but most effective sales-agent in Venice was the English Consul, Smith. His paintings were widely known here, brought back by young Englishmen as perfect souvenirs, before he himself came in 1746. He was in England for almost nine years—nearly as long as Holbein, almost exactly as long as Van Dyck. And he is at his best the supreme example of the portrait painter of places, crystallizing an austere poetry out of topographical fact. The precision of his deep perspectives was pin-pointed with the aid of a mechanical *camera*, but no such aid explains the luminous air that floods them, nor the living immediacy of his sense of place. The time is now; the salty winds crisp the water, and when you pass from the bland sunlight across the sharp edge of shadow it strikes cool. London has had no such painter before or since—Turner, Whistler, Monet and many others found their own interpretations, but no one else saw it thus, in its rare moments of complete clarity, sharp as Venice.

ANTONIO CANALETTO
Whitehall from Richmond House
1746

(left and above)
Details

It may be indeed that his eye, conditioned to the light of Venice, transposed it on to London, as later Dufy, once he had seen Mediterranean blues, managed to find them still when he returned to paler Channel waters. Scott, following close in Canaletto's footsteps in his views of London, caught perhaps more of the veil of moisture that is almost always in English skies. But Scott lacked the Venetian's spaciousness and the logic of his picture-making. Thus his view of the (now-covered) joining of the Fleet river with the Thames is at once a little shallow and a little congested, although, in his formula for indicating the ripple on the water's surface, he has borrowed straight from Canaletto (p. 53).

In 1748, Scott was prospering, and moved from the artists' quarter in London out to the most fashionable village of Twickenham. Into a former house of his at Covent Garden there moved a young and promising Welsh painter, Richard Wilson. Wilson was then starting a career as portrait painter, but in the early 'fifties he was in Italy, and there changed to what was to prove his real subject—landscape. In this switch, he was probably primarily influenced, like Scott before him, by an Italian— Zuccarelli, who had had considerable success in London with his pretty, arcadian and rather sugary Italian landscapes. In contrast, Wilson developed a stronger, more severe style, in which the classic inspiration of the two French masters of the Italian landscape is very clear: Claude and Gaspar Poussin, as also, rather later, is that of the broad shimmering golden visions of the Dutchman, Cuyp.

The *Ruins of the 'Villa of Maecenas' at Tivoli*, painted probably in Italy just before his return to England about 1758, is a fine example of the 'ruin-scape' (p. 66). The contemporary mood which they echoed is perhaps best indicated by a description of a composition by a young painter, Jonathan Skelton. Skelton was writing from Tivoli to his patron in England, perhaps in the year that Wilson painted this picture. Skelton's subject was the Grand Cascade of Tivoli—'On the right hand in the foreground is an aged Oak (as I think Mr Gray phrases it "rearing his wanton Roots so high"); under it in a pensive contemplative attitude an Old Man leaning on a Mossy Stone with a Book before him. On the left is the Temple of Concord half buried in Ruins, whose top is almost enveloped in lofty Pines, Cypresses, and Limes. To the right on the middle Ground is Coestus's Pyramidal Tomb, beyond grouping with these Ruins is the lofty Arched Temple of Peace. Behind all is a towering rocky Mountain in gloom which deprives our sight of the pleasing Skies; from

34

RICHARD WILSON Cader Idris: *Llyn-Y-Cau* c. 1770

this Mountain falls, now hid and then rising again, broad Cascades, whose general flow is the Line of Beauty; their last appearance is through the ruins of the Temple of Peace. One may draw many pleasing reflections from those venerable Relicts of ancient Roman Grandeur composed in this manner: they show how Time erases everything, for those noble and immense Edifices were certainly (by their manner of building) intended to stand for ever'.

This is redolent, as is, in its less complicated way, Wilson's canvas, of a cultivated elegiac melancholy; the literary cross-reference to Gray's poem is significant. (Wilson himself, a blunt creature, was less articulate than Skelton; his verbal response to the equally well-known falls at Terni was confined, according to legend, to a brief but splendid and justly famous apostrophe:—*Well done water, by God!*). Yet in spite of his accord with a characteristic mood of his time, back in England Wilson was never a quick-fire success, probably because he was in a way too close to the style of the great landscapists whose inspiration he reflected and renewed —but, unlike them, he was British born with a most British name, still a grave handicap as the story of West's non-buying patron indicates. Wilson's English work of the 'sixties and 'seventies, more various than is often thought, is at its best of a calm, sun-basking, poetic distinction; to

35

the English landscape he transferred something of the miraculously lucid Roman light, in which objects in the countryside can seem to group themselves consciously into a picture, as though the Almighty Himself were a painter. On other occasions (p. 35) Wilson found in the Welsh and in the English scene a radiant yet brooding tenderness, or a placid mystery of wide stretches of water, over which the eye is drawn deep into the picture to the far haze on the horizon where sight seems to melt. Such is his vision of Hounslow Heath (p. 67). Sometimes he also made a bid to align his compositions with the classic example of Claude by peopling them with classic or mythological figures, but the figures tend to be essentially extraneous in a way they are not in Claude.

Sir George Beaumont, the doyen of grand British connoisseurs at the turn of the eighteenth century into the nineteenth, once contrasted Wilson with Gainsborough in Burkian terms: Wilson represented the 'Sublime', Gainsborough the 'Beautiful'. Hence in Beaumont's opinion 'the superior popularity of Gainsborough cannot surprise us; since for one person capable of relishing the sublime, there are thousands who admire the rural and the beautiful, especially when set off by such fascinating spirit and splendour of colour as we see in the best works of Gainsborough'. For Beaumont, Wilson was of the greater intellectual and cultural calibre; the distinction between the painters reminds one of Milton's contrast of Ben Jonson's 'learned sock' with Shakespeare's 'native wood-notes wild'. Yet the most remarkable of Gainsborough's landscapes, in as much as the qualities of freshness and intuition are concerned, were probably unknown to Beaumont, and have in fact only found a full appreciation this century. These are his very early landscapes, painted in Suffolk about seventeen-fifty; strictly they are not pure landscapes as they include portraits, but the synthesis of the two genres is so perfect that the pictures become portraits of more than a person,—of a whole way of life, of a country gentry blooming modestly and naturally amongst their woods and fields, their parks and lakes. The directness of characterization is so straightforward as to seem almost naive—as if a brilliant doll-maker had learnt from Watteau (whose influence is in fact traceable in some of these paintings). The light on land and tree and water has a rainwashed brilliance, and a strange tension of stillness—sometimes it is almost a thunderlight. The *Heneage Lloyd and his Sister* is probably one of the last of this series, and in it, haunting though it is, the figures are beginning to dominate the landscape, the landscape to become an

THOMAS GAINSBOROUGH Detail, from *The Market Cart* 1786
(in colour p. 64)

accompaniment only to the figures (p. 61). He is on his way to the more conventional formula for portraiture.

In his later pure landscapes, the woodenness melts under the brush of a painter who loved the radiant shimmering fluency of his medium as perhaps no other English painter has ever done. Reynolds praised in Gainsborough 'his manner of forming all the parts of his picture together; the whole going on at the same time, in the same manner as nature creates her works'. In one of the most famous of his late landscapes, *The Market Cart* (p. 64), painted two years before he died, this 'natural' mastery is combined with an equally magnificent and fully conscious mastery of formal composition; it is painted by a man who had studied Ruysdael profoundly and learnt much from him, but the knowledge is applied direct to the English landscape, and the result retains the spontaneity of first vision—the movement of the girls in the cart and of the horse not frozen, but transposed into the movement of the brush. This is

37

the 'rural and the beautiful' at its greatest; in comparison, Wilson's views of the 'sublime', noble though they are, seem a little contrived, deliberately picturesque—scenic.

Wilson and Gainsborough form the two main peaks in eighteenth century landscape painting. But landscape was not the only alternative to portrait painting (to Gainsborough's portraits I shall come back later). Quite apart from the elusive will o' the wisp of history-painting, there was by now a fairly rewarding market for flower-pieces, still-lifes, genre pieces (scenes from contemporary life, the rustic farmyard anecdotes of which Morland was the finest practitioner; scenes from plays and so on). But for such paintings the leading connoisseurs still went to foreign sources, and it was not the leaders of taste who bought the English ones, but a humbler, more bourgeois clientele, and no major English talent was strongly enough impelled to devote himself mainly to such themes. There is no English counterpart to Chardin.

WRIGHT OF DERBY AND GEORGE STUBBS

A most interesting figure, though not a great genius, is however Joseph Wright of Derby, an able enough painter with a remarkable range of interests. He was conventionally London-trained (like Reynolds, under the society portrait painter Thomas Hudson) in portraiture, and he made the by-then conventionally necessary trip to Italy, but it was to his native Midlands that he returned in the end. In his work there comes through something of the hard-headed, practical yet romantic excitement of the dawn of the Industrial Revolution. He saw the world in a forced and sharpening light—sometimes artificial, the mill-windows brilliant in the night, faces caught in the circle of the lamp, or the red glow of an iron forge, casting monstrous shadows. This was an old trick—deriving from Caravaggio and the Dutch candlelight painters—but with it Wright brought out a sense of exploration and exploitation—scientific, intellectual and commercial, the spirit of the Midlands of his time. His patrons were men like the industrialist Arkwright of the spinning jenny, and Dr Priestley, the poetic seer of the new science (both of whom he painted).

The Experiment on a Bird in the Air-Pump, painted in 1768, is perhaps his masterpiece (p. 68). Air-pumps were then in considerable production in the Midlands, but this is not merely an excellently painted and composed study of a scientific experiment. It is raised to the pitch of a true and moving drama of life, not only by the heightening of mood by the dramatic lighting or by the subtly differentiated characterization of the participants, but by the tender yet unsentimental exploration of a human situation. The bird in the globe will die, as the vacuum is created in it; the elder girl on the right, sentimental in herself but unsentimentally drawn, cannot bear the idea and hides her face in her hands, while the younger one, though half-turned away also, looks up still to the bird with a marvellous and marvelling expression in which curiosity is just overcoming fear and pity. The haloed moon, on the edge of cloud, seen through the window on the right, adds another dimension of weirdness and mystery (Wright painted too some scenes that could serve as illustrations to the Gothick novels, like Mrs Radcliffe's, of moonlight, passion and ruins).

This is a picture that exists on many levels, and one that comes closer to the complex effect that classical or mythological history-painters were aiming at, than did any perhaps of the strictly history-paintings produced at the time. But, as they were mostly not expressed in terms of the classical culture of the age, Wright's subject pictures were for long not given their due. He himself stood apart from that culture; although he early became an Associate of the Royal Academy, he soon quarrelled with it.

George Stubbs presents in some ways a similar case: never elected a full member of the Royal Academy because his 'grading' was a low one in terms of subject-matter. He was, for his contemporaries, a mere horse-painter. In the last few years he has been much studied, and his re-assessment has lifted him to the level of the greatest of his time, the peer almost in his very different way of Reynolds and Gainsborough. His life has been fairly described as heroic. The son of a Liverpool currier, he supported himself at the beginning of his career in Northern England by painting portraits, but at the same time started in on his study of anatomy, animal and human, that was to prove not only vitally important to his art but also a new contribution to science. Stubbs was one of the great English empiricists; when he went to Rome at about the age of thirty, it was—so he is reported by a contemporary—'to convince himself that nature was and is always superior to art whether Greek or Roman—and having received this conviction he immediately resolved upon returning'. Soon afterwards occurred the episode that has most fascinated and astonished the imagination of posterity: he took a farm-house in Lincoln-

39

shire and in it, over eighteen months, he grappled with the anatomy of
the horse. His models were the decaying carcases of horses, which he
gradually stripped down, recording each revelation of anatomy in precise
and scientific drawing. The result was his book *The Anatomy of the Horse*,
a pioneering work both in science and in art.

40

GEORGE STUBBS *Mares and Foals* 1762

All his painting is based on knowledge drawn from tenacious and
ruthless study, ordered by a most precise observation and scrupulous
composition. In the 'seventies, his scientific interests shifted from anatomy

GEORGE STUBBS Detail, from *The Hambletonian* 1799 or 1800

to chemistry, and helped by Wedgwood, the enlightened founder of the great pottery firm, he experimented in enamel painting. But his associations with high fashion in culture (one is almost tempted to write, unfairly, *haute couture*) were always cool; he had ambitions to succeed as portrait painter and as history painter, which were never fulfilled, and he died in old age far from well off. His true and great originality was not on conventional lines, and could not be grasped by contemporary taste.

42

His is a more austere, more purely pictorial, more naked poetry than that of any other English painter, and can at its best attain a still, self-sufficient monumentality—most remarkably perhaps in the famous life-size painting of the race horse *Hambletonian* with its groom. His portrait of a *Lady and Gentleman in a Carriage* may seem at first sight no more than another, admittedly fine, example of the outdoor conversation pieces, often involving animals, that were popular at the time (p. 69). But comparison with an excellent but conventional example of one of these underlines Stubbs' exceptional qualities.

Take for example Johann Zoffany's *Family Group in a Landscape* in the Tate Gallery (p. 71). He was a German-born painter with Italian experience, a founder-member of the Royal Academy, who specialized in England in the conversation piece, whether of actors in scenes from stage-plays (he was a friend of Garrick's) or straightforward family groups. While lacking the satiric verve of Hogarth, he was of an enviable and delightful professional ability, yet his group, compared with Stubbs', remains only on the level of anecdotery; all is affection, good humour, romp and charm, but as a pictorial unity there is little coherence. It is a collection of single figures ranged agreeably across the foreground, free in colour and gesture, and lively, if a little obvious, in characterization, but entirely lacking in what might be called a classic inevitability. It is an artistic contrivance. In contrast the silence of the Stubbs is superb. Here there is no anecdotal interest; nothing is forced and the picture is balanced delicately as scales on the central vertical of the poplars in the background. The painting of the intricacies of the carriage is not a mere *tour-de-force* of painstaking realism, but is subordinate to the movement of the picture: the two figures, leaning slightly in the seat, echo the outward tilt of the wheels. The magnificent sleek black animals balance the human figures and the carriage; everything is characterized with a sort of detached, precise passion and informed by an exact knowledge of the physical structure of each object. Stubbs' hard-won first-hand experience of anatomy is reflected in his pictures; they too have a rigorous essential anatomy, an organic structure behind them that gives them a logic unmatched in English painting. In the Lincolnshire farmhouse, he had served an apprenticeship similar in kind though not in method to that of the apprentice in an Italian painter's workshop in the Renaissance, and on such a discipline rests the unfumbling classic sureness of his touch and of his art of picture-building.

43

THE HON. GEORGE TOWNSHEND
AFTERWARDS
1 VISCOUNT TOWNSHEND

THOMAS HUDSON *Marquis Townshend* 1759

SIR JOSHUA REYNOLDS

Hogarth, Wright, Stubbs—all artists wrongly or under-estimated by their contemporaries—are now revealed stripped of the conventions of their times in what seems a truer perspective. In contrast, consider now the artist who was in full accord with his times and honoured by them as no English artist had been honoured before—Sir Joshua Reynolds. Unlike Stubbs, he has, at present, somewhat depreciated, if you consider him purely as artist; yet, as a sort of historical monument, as an embodiment of his age, he still stands central and commanding and admirable in our eyes upon his eminence. However much one may probe his weaknesses, however much his work may seem, in the last analysis, to lack that urgency that lifts the heart, one cannot but admire the more, the more one studies his work.

Unlike Stubbs, or Wright, or even Gainsborough, he seems to have had all the advantages. Socially he was impeccably successful, consorting as respectful equal not only with the aristocracy of birth but with the still fabulous aristocracy of merit of that remarkable age: the intimate of Dr Johnson and of Burke, the befriender of Goldsmith. In his own sphere, the head of the profession: first President, and in large part begetter, of the Royal Academy, knight and an honorary Doctor of the University of Oxford. He was prosperous to a reasonable affluence; he was even successful as a man of letters, a theorist, able to support his practice with a reasoned and general philosophy nobly set out in a prose not unworthy of a friend of Johnson's; Reynolds, amongst so many other things, made art-criticism respectable in England. Moreover personally he had great dignity, charm and urbanity.

Yet he was not born to most of these advantages; in his ambition and by his own capacity he created them, and his triumph is that of a remarkable but not intrinsically outstanding ability developed to its utmost by hard work and persistence and intelligence, and fired by an unfailing devotion to the art which he served. His training was orthodox enough, under the best master of society portraiture as it was then understood: Thomas Hudson. But there was perhaps only one lesson relevant to Reynolds' particular talent that Hudson could have taught him, and that lesson unfortunately Reynolds did not heed: the necessity of a sound technique in painting (many of Reynolds' paintings are now but ghosts of their original selves, owing to his irresponsible experimentation with techniques). To understand the extent of the revolution that Reynolds was to bring about, a word on the situation that he found upon his arrival on the scene in the seventeen-forties is necessary. It was, in brief, a *status quo;* society portraiture had become a monotonous repetition of the same theme with only the most limited of variations permissible. According to the formula, the sitter was to be posed centrally, with the background (curtain, pillar, chair, perhaps a hint of landscape) disposed like a backdrop behind; normally the head was done by the master, the body by a pupil or 'drapery assistant' who might serve several painters. Pose and expression, even the features themselves, tended to be regulated to a standard of polite and inexpressive elegance; the portraits told little about their subjects other than that they were that sort of people who had their portraits painted—they gave nothing away beyond the summary description of the features. They were effigies; life has departed (p. 44).

Before Reynolds there were certain stirrings of revolt. Allan Ramsay, whose early portraits of the 'forties can be sometimes confused with those by Hudson (although Ramsay had a lightness of touch unknown to Hudson), was capable of far subtler variations than most. In some ways he even forestalled Reynolds, and in his best later work (sometimes influenced by Reynolds' example) he rivalled him. Indeed, in his later portraits, in one aspect, compared with the earlier works of Reynolds, he was superior to the younger man. As Horace Walpole justly remarked— 'Mr Reynolds seldom succeeds in women, Mr Ramsay is formed to paint them' (the criticism does not apply by any means to some of Reynolds' later female portraits). That was in 1759; Ramsay's portrait of his wife, (p. 65), dates from about that time. It is a silvery, cool-hued picture of the most elegant informality, with a conviction of live, easy intimacy that is a world away from Hudson and his school, and which, in simplicity, in warmth perhaps of discrete affection, is beyond the range of anything Reynolds ever painted. But a few years after this Ramsay found royal favour (almost the one worldly blessing denied to Reynolds), and the last twenty years of his life were spent in agreeable idleness, his main painting concern being the supervision of the production of royal state-portraits by assistants.

The more complex of Ramsay's portraits, however, occur relatively rarely in his work, and the revolution which they foreshadow was only realised by Reynolds. It was Reynolds who insisted in his practice that a

46   SIR JOSHUA REYNOLDS Detail, from *General Tarleton* 1782

portrait could and should be also a full, complex work of art on many levels; he conceived his portraits in terms of history-painting. Each fresh sitter was not just a physical fact to be recorded, but rather a story to be told (or sometimes, one suspects, a myth to be created). His people are no longer static, but caught between this movement and the next, between one moment and the next. Their minds and bodies exist on the brink of various possibilities, and they are essentially involved in the weather of life. Sometimes they seem like actors, pausing in soliloquy (p. 108). Reynolds was indeed a consummate producer of characters (whether they bore much resemblance to the originals, the raw stuff from which they were created, is another, academic, matter; in point of fact, the catching of a convincing likeness was not his forte), and his production methods reward investigation. For them he called upon the full repertoire of the Old Masters; in Italy, as a young man, he had studied the old masters of all schools, not so that he could ape their individual works, but in order to win a similar mastery of the effects which they knew how to achieve: to rival them in their own language but not to pastiche them. In his broad, broken handling of colour, and in the fat and sensuous texture of his paint, he recalls the sixteenth century Venetians. In his building up of the picture in light and shade, his handling of the intrinsic drama of a composition, he also paid homage to Rembrandt. In the actual design, he had the whole Italian school, as an inexhaustible well, to draw upon. In his conception of the grand, the heroic, the sublime, he came more and more to invoke the spirit of Michelangelo. But all these contributions would have availed nothing— would on the contrary have been disastrous—if he had not possessed, in the first place, a mental and visual digestive ability of amazing capacity, and, secondly, a beautifully just feeling for composition. As it was, by his example he established English portraiture as a branch of painting of a similar kind to, and comparable with, the work of the Old Masters.

In fact he was avowedly what is called an eclectic, but on the whole justifiably. One of the primary requisites 'in our *Poet*, or Maker' (this is Ben Jonson, writing a century and a half earlier) 'is Imitation, to be able to convert the substance, or Riches of another *Poet*, to his own use . . . Not to imitate servilely; but to draw forth out of the best and choicest of flowers, with the Bee, and turn all into Honey'. This is a classic statement of the academic case; the danger is of course that originality may be under-estimated (as it was by Reynolds), and that students following

48

HANS EWORTH. SIR JOHN LUTTRELL. 1550. Luttrell Collection, Dunster Castle

NICHOLAS HILLIARD. UNKNOWN YOUTH. c. 1590.
Victoria and Albert Museum, London

WILLIAM DOBSON. Endymion Porter. c. 1642. Tate Gallery, London

PETER LELY. Two Ladies of the Lake Family. c. 1660. Tate Gallery, London

52

SAMUEL SCOTT. Entrance to the Fleet River. c. 1750. Guildhall Art Gallery, London

53

WILLIAM HOGARTH. THE RAKE'S PROGRESS II: THE LEVEE. c. 1732. Sir John Soane's Museum, London

54

WILLIAM HOGARTH. Lord George Graham in his Cabin. c. 1745. National Maritime Museum, London

WILLIAM HOGARTH. CAPTAIN THOMAS CORAM. 1740.

Thomas Coram Foundation for Children, London

WILLIAM HOGARTH. An Election III: The Polling. c. 1754. Sir John Soane's Museum, London

JOSHUA REYNOLDS. LADY COCKBURN AND HER THREE ELDEST SONS. 1773.
National Gallery, London

JOSHUA REYNOLDS. Colonel George K. H. Coussmaker. 1782.

Metropolitan Museum of Art, New York

JOSHUA REYNOLDS. SELF-PORTRAIT. c. 1773. Royal Academy of Arts, London

THOMAS GAINSBOROUGH. Heneage Lloyd and his Sister. c. 1750. Fitzwilliam Museum, Cambridge

61

THOMAS GAINSBOROUGH. MARY, COUNTESS HOWE. c. 1765.

Iveagh Bequest, Kenwood

THOMAS GAINSBOROUGH. SELF-PORTRAIT. 1787.
Royal Academy of Arts, London

THOMAS GAINSBOROUGH. THE MARKET CART. 1786. Tate Gallery, London

ALLAN RAMSAY. THE ARTIST'S WIFE. c. 1755. National Gallery of Scotland, Edinburgh

RICHARD WILSON. Ruins of the 'Villa of Maecenas' at Tivoli. c. 1757.

Tate Gallery, London

RICHARD WILSON. ON HOUNSLOW HEATH. c. 1770. Tate Gallery, London

67

JOSEPH WRIGHT OF DERBY. EXPERIMENT WITH THE AIR-PUMP. c. 1768. Tate Gallery, London

GEORGE STUBBS. A LADY AND GENTLEMAN IN A CARRIAGE. 1787. National Gallery, London

69

HENRY RAEBURN. LIEUTENANT-COLONEL BRYCE McMURDO.
National Gallery, London

JOHANN ZOFFANY. A FAMILY GROUP IN A LANDSCAPE. c. 1775. Tate Gallery, London

71

FRANCIS TOWNE. Source of the Arveyron. 1781.

Victoria and Albert Museum, London

The Drunken Husband

THOMAS ROWLANDSON. THE DRUNKEN HUSBAND. British Museum, London

74

THOMAS ROWLANDSON. Bridge at Knaresborough, Yorkshire. 1807. Victoria and Albert Museum, London

THOMAS GIRTIN. RUE SAINT-DENIS. c. 1802. Sir Edmund Bacon, Bt., Norwich

THOMAS LAWRENCE. Queen Charlotte. c. 1790.

National Gallery, London

THOMAS LAWRENCE. ELIZABETH FARREN. 1790.
Metropolitan Museum of Art, New York

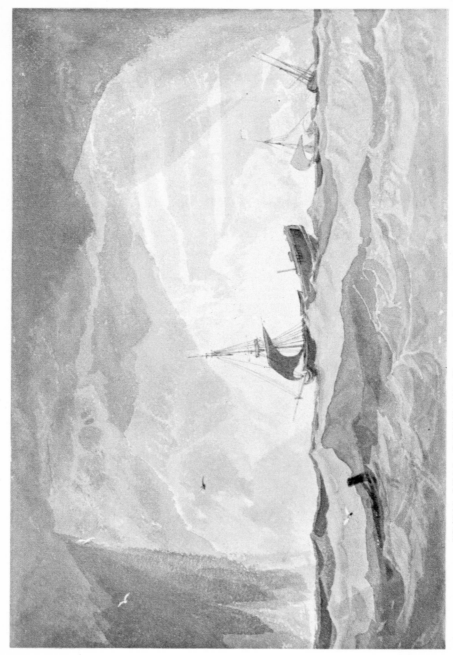

JOHN SELL COTMAN. DISMASTED BRIG. c. 1823. British Museum, London

JOHN CONSTABLE. DEDHAM MILL. 1820. *Victoria and Albert Museum, London*

JOHN CONSTABLE. BRIGHTON BEACH WITH COLLIERS. 1824. Victoria and Albert Museum, London

80

JOHN CONSTABLE. A COUNTRY LANE. c. 1826. Tate Gallery, London

JOHN CONSTABLE. VIEW AT EPSOM. c. 1808. Tate Gallery, London

ICHARD PARKES BONINGTON. A SCENE IN NORMANDY. c. 1820. National Gallery, London

83

WILLIAM BLAKE. Adam and Eve and the Angel. 1808. Museum of Fine Arts, Boston

84

JOSEPH MALLORD WILLIAM TURNER. GRAND CANAL, VENICE. 1835.

Metropolitan Museum of Art, New York

JOSEPH MALLORD WILLIAM TURNER. Burning of the Houses of Parliament. 1835.

Philadelphia Museum of Art

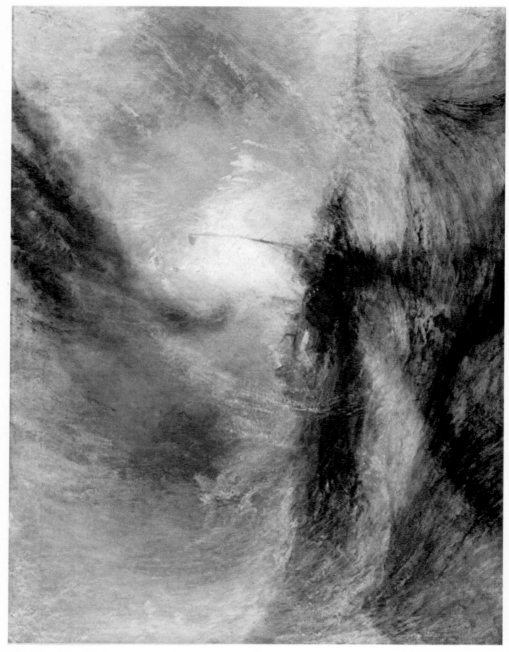

JOSEPH MALLORD WILLIAM TURNER. SNOWSTORM. 1842. National Gallery, London

JOSEPH MALLORD WILLIAM TURNER. BELLINZONA FROM THE SOUTH. 1841. British Museum, London

SAMUEL PALMER. CORNFIELD BY MOONLIGHT. c. 1830. Sir Kenneth Clark Collection

90

SAMUEL PALMER. View at Tivoli. c. 1839. Philadelphia Museum of Art

91

GEORGE FREDERICK WATTS. SELF-PORTRAIT AS A YOUNG MAN. 1834.

Watts Gallery, Compton, Guildford

FORD MADOX BROWN. CARRYING CORN. 1854. Tate Gallery, London

93

ARTHUR HUGHES. THE TRYST. c. 1854. Tate Gallery, London

AMES ABBOT McNEILL WHISTLER. ARRANGEMENT IN GREY AND BLACK. 1871. Louvre, Paris

WALTER GREAVES. Hammersmith Bridge on Boat-Race Day. c. 1862. Tate Gallery, London

96

in the tradition may become paralysed by dependence on authority and dogma.

It may be asked why, if Reynolds thought the greatest achievement in painting to be history-painting, he did not apply himself to it. He did, but not as his means of livelihood, because he could not have lived off it; in his practice but not in his theory (in his *Discourses*), he admitted that the traditional history-picture was no longer historically valid for his times; his solution, in marrying the history-picture to the portrait, was a brilliant and most English compromise; none of his history-pictures, the *Death of Dido* and all the many others, is in fact as satisfactory, nor 'works' as well as any of his finest portraits.

In the first example of his work reproduced, *Lady Cockburn and her Sons*, his production methods can be studied in depth (p. 58). The poses stir memories of the Carracci and of Rubens, the sumptuous red hangings echo Van Dyck, and the conception of the figure, the theme, has been related to the popular Italian subject of Charity, and is perhaps traceable back to Michelangelo. As if this was not enough for undertones and overtones, when the picture was engraved it was titled, not with the sitter's name (which was Augusta Ann) but as *Cornelia and her children*, Cornelia being the mother of the Roman heroes, the Gracchi (the brilliant macaw whose reds so boldly come to near-clash with those of the draperies, has a more simple explanation, being a studio prop of Reynolds' that used to perch alarmingly on visitors' shoulders). The picture is ably, even nobly realized, and much of its high cultural implications would have been recognizable by (or explainable to) the sitter and client, flattering her further by setting her so firmly amongst classics; yet the taste of more recent times may well be jarred by something in this picture that seems close to affectation. It is in a key, a mode of sentiment, with which most of us are no longer in tune. And it is probably true to say that Reynolds was, in this case, exaggerating somewhat; it comes from his most classicizing period, the 'seventies, when he was striving to make his pictures as rich as possible. It is very much a 'public' picture, painted with exhibition specifically in mind in the newly founded artists' display ground at the Academy (it was shown there in 1774), and designed to compel the spectators' attention to itself, to the detraction of the works of his rivals.

Later, he reverted to simpler compositions, though behind them there lies an ever-increasing experience and knowledge. Such is the whole length of *Colonel Coussmaker* of 1782, a relatively simple but immensely subtle and fluent study in curves and echoing angles: a portrait of extraordinary relaxation and breeding, yet balanced as lightly and crisply as a hair-spring (p. 59). Surely few people can resist the sheer pleasure of this, and it may remind one of a remark Reynolds made in his apprentice days when writing home about his painting—'While I am doing this I am the happiest creature in the world.'

The *Self-Portrait* on the other hand speaks admirably and eloquently of the high seriousness of the great artist; he appears not as mere painter, but as the official representative of Art (p. 60). Wearing his D.C.L. gown with senatorial dignity that recalls Titian, accompanied by a bust of Michelangelo, and enhanced by a mystery of light out of darkness that certainly owes much to Rembrandt, he presents himself nevertheless— with full confidence but not in arrogance—in that superb decorum which was one of his characteristics. Compared with Rembrandt, it lacks inwardness and depth, and that magical fusion of flesh and spirit of the Dutchman's late self-portraits. But if it be true that Reynolds was not great among the greatest as was Rembrandt, nevertheless this noble portrait is of very high order, and expresses the best and most serious in its painter. For all his theory, he was ultimately an English empiricist, resting secure on the proven and individual fact—the individual presence of each fresh sitter whence, each time, a fresh start had to be made.

GAINSBOROUGH'S PORTRAITS

Thomas Gainsborough was Reynolds' rival and almost exact contemporary. He was also his almost exact opposite, although the often-made contention that neither influenced the other in their painting is overstated: Gainsborough surely owed much to the immense widening of scope that Reynolds' 'damned Variousness' had created for the portrait-painter, while Reynolds' *Colonel Coussmaker* would never have had quite that fluent grace, I suspect, if he had never known Gainsborough's later work. I have already touched upon Gainsborough's early portraiture— that mingling of portraiture and landscape which he abandoned when he left Suffolk, about 1760, for the more sophisticated clientele of Bath. There he, as Reynolds had before him, turned to the Old Masters, but primarily to only one of them, and not to an Italian (he never visited

THOMAS GAINSBOROUGH Detail, from *Lady Howe* (in colour p. 62)

Italy)—but to Van Dyck. To this study he brought an innate genius for drawing that Reynolds never possessed, and a sensuous delight in colour and movement that seems at times to amount almost to intoxication with them. No other painter has thus caught the essence of silks and lace in motion, nor the tremulous flicker of an eyelash. In contrast to Reynolds', the essence of his genius was intuitive, and he profits far less from commentary; his art develops freely according to his own genius, the touch of the brush getting ever lighter, the atmosphere ever more aerial (p. 63). To appreciate one of his great masterpieces, one does not need to have the likeness of his mood with that of Watteau, or the hint of *chinoiserie* in the delicately absurd hat, harped upon over much; one merely needs eyes to see with and enough life left to fall in love. Gainsborough is the purest lyricist of our painters; Reynolds the master of the epic style.

The *Lady Howe* portrait (p. 62) was painted fairly early in his Bath period, about 1765; that is at a time when he had achieved a remarkable balance between the demands of the almost liquid urgency of his style and the necessity of combining with it a record of the minute detail that fixed the likeness of his subject. In his later style—the famous *Morning Walk* in the National Gallery is one of the finest examples of it—the sitters seem to merge one into another as though faces in a happy dream.

ROMANTICISM

Towards the close of the eighteenth century, all over Europe, the tensions that had gradually built up behind the decorous, bewigged facade of the Age of Reason reached breaking point, and burst in revolution. The most violent manifestation was of course the French Revolution, followed by the wars that burned intermittently through Europe for the next twenty years. But this was too a period of less bloodily violent yet equally far-reaching revolutions in other spheres: in industry and commerce, the Industrial Revolution, that accelerated the change in social life to a remarkable pitch. And in art likewise, the Romantic Revolution.

Romanticism perennially escapes definition—it has so many aspects, some of which can be discerned in the most classical of classic art. As its most perspicacious commentator, Baudelaire, observed: 'Romanticism is precisely situated neither in choice of subjects nor in exact truth, but in a mode of feeling'. In fact, however elusive its definition may be, it is obvious beyond doubt that there was a fundamental shift in the nature of artistic expression at the time, and Baudelaire's remark at least points to the most important quality of this shift: the motive force becomes emotion rather than reason. This does not, as is sometimes suggested, mean that reason was thrown overboard, but that it was inspired and illuminated by emotion. This helps one to understand a seeming paradox in much romantic art, when it appears to possess both near- and far-sight. Reynolds, somewhere in his *Discourses*, described 'the disposition to abstractions, to generalizing and classification' as 'the great glory of the human mind'; this remark provoked anathema from Blake in the margins of his copy of Reynolds' work: 'To Generalize is to be an Idiot; to particularize is the alone Distinction of Merit'. Again and again one finds the romantic artist dwelling, doting on the particular, the detail, the minute—as Constable, for example, in his meticulously observed portraits of individual trees; yet the intensity of such contemplation finds in the exact detail intimations of a larger order, even of immortality. 'To see a World in a Grain of Sand, And a Heaven in a Wild Flower'. In the eighteenth century, the mean—the scale—had been set by the human figure, particularly in England, and the most significant art perhaps had been the portraiture of men and women. For the Romantics, the scale became superhuman; the scope of the body could not contain human passion, and it found its expression in all nature. An early critic of Turner, in 1799, was on the mark: 'Turner's views are not mere ordinary transcripts of nature; he always throws some peculiar and striking *character* into the scene he represents'. The sea in storm and calm, the vast movement of sky and cloud just as the dewdrop shining on the leaf, all become the expression, the symbols even, of man's desires and sorrows and doubts. The finite is only the microcosm of the infinite; a pool of rainwater after a shower postulates the whole sky, and heaven itself.

One danger is, of course, once the human scale is abandoned, that all proportion may be lost. Blake, walking a tightrope in mid-air amongst his teeming visions and with the hard earth beneath, crazy as a saint, sometimes seems to have lost all sense of proportion (without which one cannot communicate one's vision to other mortals). The true balance was held by Constable. (He, it is said, only met Blake once, when Blake was roused to enthusiasm by his drawings, crying: 'Why, this is not drawing, but *inspiration!'*—to which Constable replied: 'I never knew it before; I meant it for drawing'.) Constable indeed, who is on record as saying that, for him, feeling was only another word for painting, also said: 'In such an age as this, painting should be *understood*, not looked on with blind wonder, nor considered only as a poetic inspiration, but as a pursuit, *legitimate, scientific*, and *mechanical'*.

But the wonder was certainly there: no blind rapture, but a passionate scrutiny, seeking the exact lineaments even of the infinite, that favourite romantic aspiration. 'Cursed be the picture that shows nothing beyond the finite,' wrote Delacroix, 'the merit of a picture is the indefinable; precisely that which escapes precision'. To achieve which one must proceed with almost surgical subtlety: one thinks of the earth melting into the colours of the prism, into light, in Turner's visions.

Romanticism was a European movement in art, but in it for the first time for centuries, with Constable and Turner especially, and with Lawrence in his manner, English artists led the way. But before coming to these great figures, we must glance, though only too briefly, at a peculiarly English achievement that was to prove particularly congenial to the romantic search: the work of the watercolourists.

THE WATERCOLOURISTS

Watercolour, so swift to use, so delicate, so portable, and so comparatively ephemeral compared with the solid painting of oilcolours, is especially suited to catch just those ephemeral effects in nature with which the Romantics were so fascinated. Through the eighteenth century the medium became popular and widespread, but to begin with was used mainly for topographical purposes—to take the portrait, to make a record of a particular place: a patron's house, a special view. They were also mostly more tinted drawings than paintings; colour was subordinate, and generally from a very limited palette, often almost monochrome, used as a wash to give substance and relief to the line. With the work of Paul Sandby however, though he was trained as a strict record-taking topographer, a far greater vivacity and richness was introduced, and colour becomes no longer a mere fill in—Sandby drew often not with the pencil, but with the brush.

The contribution of Francis Towne is a most individual variation on what might be called the opposite tradition in watercolour to that practised by Sandby: the counterpart of ideal landscape painting in oils, an interpretation, in poetic, elegiac terms rather than those of strict topography. In such watercolours the traveller recorded the picturesque wherever he came across it. The most influential document to tune English sensibilities to landscape for its own self was Thomson's famous poem *The Seasons;* as early as 1726, in his preface to *Winter*, he locates the poet's delight as in 'the wild, romantic county'. Writing in 1782 (the year after the Towne drawing shown on page 72 was made), the critic Warton indicated which aspects of nature had by then proved to be of particular appeal: 'The *Seasons* of Thomson have been very instrumental in diffusing a general taste for the beauties of *nature* and *landscape*. It is only within a few years that the picturesque scenes of our own country, our lakes, mountains, cascades, caverns and castles have been visited and described . . .' In his choice of wild mountain scenery for subject then Towne was typical of many watercolourists of his time; it is a fascination of course that was intensified in the generation of the Lakeist poets, and one that still has not lost its force. The manner of his description is however very personal; though the outlines are lucidly traced in the topographical manner, and the colour is a little flat and pale,

ALEXANDER COZENS *The Cloud*

the generalization of the natural forms into what, so it appears to modern eyes, is close to an abstract pattern, is unlike that of any other artist of the time, and achieves something of the strange visionary quality of Blake's world. A primaeval world of a frozen yet fluid geometry, composed in a beautiful balance of broad contrasting tones; no other painter has succeeded in suggesting the *movement* of a glacier beneath its monumental seeming-immobility.

The enlargement of the possibilities of the medium that the work of Sandby and of Towne indicates are considerable, but less fundamental than that to which Sandby's contemporary, Alexander Cozens, and his son J. R. Cozens, pointed in their practice. The elder Cozens, in a work first published in 1759 as *An Essay to facilitate the invention of Landskips*, suggests an entirely new freedom. While on the one hand sensitive to the particular atmosphere of a particular time of day or effect of weather (noting occasionally on his drawings, much as Constable was to do later,

103

comments such as 'before rain', or 'intermixture of clouds with the landscape'), he already is concerned with another approach typical of
romantic landscape, by which it can become almost pure invention of
the painter, a subjective mood manifested in rocks and trees, in sky and
cloud and shadow. He was the inventor of the notorious 'blottesques':
free compositions made by elaborating designs from a spatter of blots
and dashes in Indian ink thrown on the paper. Here we have the principle
of accident and intuition introduced into English art, and another principle which was to be formally set out by the connoisseur Richard Payne
Knight in the 'nineties: that what moves us in a work of art is not the
subject matter, objective qualities in the thing seen, so much as 'light,
variously gradated and modified' and the subjective associations that the
painting aroused in the mind of the spectator. Such a view tends to
distinguish, to separate out the purely visual qualities of a painting
irrespective of its subject matter, and from it the ultimate development
to a purely abstract art of design and colour is logical. In some of Cozens'
work too the romantic symbols of the infinite, sky and sea, and dizzy
contrast of deepest shadow against dazzling light, are already stressed,
and even in his more conventional ideal landscapes, unpeopled, there
are echoes of lonely immensity.

One of the most remarkable of English draughtsmen however was still
working in an essentially older technique. Thomas Rowlandson is in fact
more draughtsman than watercolourist; his use of wash colour is strictly
to enhance his cavorting line, and the only quality for which he might
be suspected of romantic leanings, is his unwearying devotion to sheer
excess. Most of his innumerable drawings are of course on the borderline
of caricature (p. 73), if not over it, and he must stand here as representative of the brilliant school of English caricaturists of his time. One of
these, James Gillray, primarily a political cartoonist and of the first rank
as such, was also a true romantic expressionist in that the follies and vices
of his creatures are not merely displayed but warp and contort their
shapes till they seem to personify themselves. Unlike Gillray, or Hogarth,
Rowlandson was rarely satirical in a didactic or a political way; he was
content simply to upset the apple-cart, and did so with exuberant talent.
For him the decorum of Reynolds existed to be turned upside down, so
displaying usually enormous thighs and harvest-moon buttocks in a skirl
of skirts; he is no artist for the faint-hearted. Here there is no cry of
protest at the folly or the absurdity of the human breed, but simply a

JAMES GILLRAY *George Humphreys* 1811

delighted record of that folly and absurdity in their most extravagant
shape, their vitality matched only by the vitality, curvetting like a
bouncing rubber ball, of his draughtsmanship. Much of the same exuberance appears in his rarer landscape drawings; these are rural picturesque scenes, close in mood and characterization to the farmscapes in
oils of his friend Morland: a plump land full of plump rustics and plump
animals, but seen with a brisk freshness of vision and the irresistible
rhythm of contour that runs through all his work, although his summary
treatment of detail (see especially his formula for trees) is confined to
the old convention (p. 74).

The full transition of the eighteenth century watercolour into the
nineteenth century manner is epitomized in the development of the
brilliant, brief-lived Thomas Girtin, who died in 1802 in his twenty-
eighth year. His early work dealt with strictly accurate topography,
drawings of architectural subjects made for an antiquary. But by 1795
he was working, with Turner, his exact contemporary, copying from

105

Cozens and other masters in the house of the collector and patron, Dr. Monro, who seems to have run what almost amounted to an academy for young artists. With astonishing speed the young artist matured, and his range widened; he travelled extensively, and in the last five years of his life he achieved for the English watercolour a new independence, in which directness of observation was matched and inspired by a magnificent pictorial imagination that discarded worn-out conventions of composition.

Girtin's view of the *Rue St.-Denis* reproduced here (p. 75) is a late work, and relates to a series of views of Paris that he made in 1801. This is very far from being an exact architectural description; rather, it becomes a sort of triumphant architectural blues, in procession up the street to the great climax of the arch. The windows and doorways, the flagpoles, become not so much details of buildings as an almost musical notation, flickering and dancing along the broad areas of colour. Another version of this composition shows the street crowded with figures; here, emptied of human beings, it becomes its own sufficient drama, the street deep and sheer as a canyon, yet advancing inexorably up its perspective to vanishing point (the drawing is said to have served as design for a back-cloth at one of the London theatres). Girtin and Turner, born in the same year, were in their beginnings almost twin geniuses, although the more restless ambition of Turner was evident even then. Though Turner's remark—'If Girtin had lived, I should have starved'—is probably apocryphal, it indicates justly the stature of his rival's brief-lived talent, narrower perhaps than Turner's, but less wayward, with a most pure and direct impact.

With Turner and Girtin, as leading landscape draughtsmen about 1800, was ranked John Sell Cotman, the Norfolk painter; though towards the end of his career he lost favour, his are now amongst the popular and beloved watercolours. If sometimes he carried Girtin's delight in contrasts of sharply silhouetted masses of colour to a rather over-schematized degree, he had always a remarkably sure feeling for composition, for a superbly decorative design, and his technique was of a wonderfully crisp brilliance and facility. In the *Dismasted Brig* (p. 78), painted at a time of crisis about 1823, his technique is seen at its most accomplished, the helplessness of the stricken ship—a theme to which Romantic painters returned again and again—contrasted with, and emphasized by, the firm design that controls the chaos of the storm. It is

106

one of the most haunting of English watercolours; Cotman nevertheless had the chagrin of seeing it sold at auction in 1836 for seventeen shillings.

By the time of Cotman's death, in 1842, the watercolour had for some time been fully established as a work of art in its own right, and with its proper place no longer only in the portfolios and the drawing-books, but in gilt frames on the walls. In 1797, Dr Monro had 90 drawings framed on the walls of his parlour, and 120 in the drawing room—of course, Monro was a specialist collector, but this gives an idea of the impending popularity of the art. For the more modest house, for those many patrons who, although they may not have owned staterooms of country-house grandeur, nevertheless owned villas of substance and comfort, the water-colour was the natural form of decoration.

LAWRENCE AND PORTRAITURE

Baudelaire, writing in 1846 about portraiture, distinguished between two kinds: one which can be understood as 'history', such as that practised by David and Ingres; the other described as 'fictional' and 'romantic'. The masters of the latter sort whom he selected were Rembrandt—and Reynolds and Sir Thomas Lawrence. Their method implied the translation of a picture into a poem—'a poem with all its accessories, a poem full of space and reverie'. It is perhaps unexpected to find Reynolds classified as a great 'romantic' painter, yet, whatever his precepts, his effects, particularly in some of his latest portraits, are romantic: for example, in his portrait of the aged but titanic soldier, Lord Heathfield (in the National Gallery), the whole picture becomes what Coleridge might have called an 'organic' extension of the sitter's character and achievement, a victorious serenity shining through the murk of war; this is more an expression of feeling than a descriptive painting (p. 108).

Most of the portraitists who worked in the fifty years after Reynolds death in 1792 were content to perform within the vastly enlarged scope that he had given to the art; none however matched his stature, and few produced variations of any great novelty or significance upon his themes. Raeburn was one who did; obsessed by light, he was capable of almost hallucinatory visions such as that, now at Edinburgh (the study for the portrait of his son on a pony), in which his sitters seem almost to float,

SIR JOSHUA REYNOLDS *Lord Heathfield* 1787

translucent and aerial, in reflected light and shadow. But more generally he favoured this light fiercely focused to emphasize the character of his sitters in their faces. His clientele was mostly Scottish, and almost all his life he worked in Edinburgh, recording with a broad, crisp and lively naturalism the forthright countenances of its burghers. In the background of the wholelength of *Colonel McMurdo* (p. 70), a wild Scottish trout-stream is agreeably indicated, but the fusion of the sitter with it is hardly complete; lit searchingly with indoor studio lighting, the head and shoulders are out of key and mood with the rest of the picture. Raeburn was perhaps at his best when confronted by the faces of the very old; then his account of the experience scored by time upon the human face is often both searching and brilliant.

The true successor to Reynolds was Thomas Lawrence, and Reynolds recognized him as such when the young prodigy was barely twenty. Two of the pictures reproduced here, exhibited in the Academy of 1790, were painted probably in Lawrence's twenty-first year; owing much to Reynolds, they have also a sort of nervous sensitivity and a sensuous elegance of paint that are quite foreign to the older master. *Queen Charlotte*, (p. 76) an opportunity for success and name-making grasped with astounding confidence by the young painter, shows his technique already almost fully formed, and is also of heart-lifting freshness in approach to so formal a subject; the rather elderly Queen's face is treated with decent respect, but the sheer elegance and the poise herald the revival of court portraiture that Lawrence was to accomplish—a vision of aristocracy that in mood goes back to Van Dyck rather than Reynolds. Like Van Dyck, Lawrence was a courtier-painter, and it was the most eminent figures of his time who were to precipitate his finest masterpieces, the set of portraits of the victorious allied statesmen that he painted after Waterloo and which now adorn the Waterloo Chamber at Windsor Castle. But he was also a consummate painter, not so much of women *per se*, as of the romance of woman. The whole-length of *Eliza Farren* (p. 77) is a stunning document of romance, and its sitter almost an epitome of his talent; she was an actress who married into the aristocracy (she became Countess of Derby). Throughout his work, Lawrence tended to depict the aristocracy in the light of an essentially stage glamour. He himself was a keen amateur actor, and intimate friend of the Siddonses and the Kembles; perhaps because he was so deeply in sympathy with the theatre, his portraits, theatrical though they are, at their best (Lawrence like all

109

SIR THOMAS LAWRENCE Detail, from *Captain Graham Moore* 1792

English portraitists painted too much and his work is very uneven) come across with fresh and living conviction; if his sitters seem to be putting on a show, they do it with conviction, body and soul, and project across the footlights a heightened version of themselves. Miss Farren is perhaps acting a little the part of a lady of high degree (what is she doing in *those* clothes, dewy as gossamer though they be, out in the fields?), but no one will deny that she carries it off. The painter Northcote (a rival, and doubtless jealous) once described Lawrence as a 'man-milliner sort of painter, a meteor of fashion'; in part the criticism is just, but it also underlines Lawrence's real achievement and relevance; for him, clothes, in the fluent brilliant sheen of his paint, become a necessary extension of his sitter, as though plumage of birds of paradise. He revealed romanticism in the drawingroom; it must be remembered—and Lawrence does not fail to remind you—that he was the visual stage-manager of Regency society, one of the most sophisticated periods ever known, and the prophets of that society were on the one hand the slightly demonic mysterious figure of Byron, and on the other, the austere and perfect silhouette of the arch-Dandy, Brummell, for whom the problem of one's physical presentation in society was almost one of metaphysics.

CONSTABLE

Lawrence's achievement is perhaps now underrated (is this from a puritan distrust of a supreme cunning of the hand?), and the three Romantic geniuses usually placed head and shoulders above their contemporaries are Constable, Turner and Blake. They are so essentially different one from the other that it is difficult to compare their stature. Such comparisons are in any case idle except when they shed light on the figures concerned; Constable himself once said that 'it is difficult to establish superiority in these things', going on to quote a remark of Opie's about Titian, to the effect that Titian, though perhaps not the best painter in the world, produced the best pictures. It is a comment that applies, reversed, almost to Constable himself; if somehow, unaccountably, he did not produce the greatest paintings in English art, he is still the greatest of English painters.

One of the difficulties about Constable is that of seeing his work objectively; once you have come into contact with Constable the man, it is very hard to see his work other than in the sympathetic light of admiration and friendship. He was quite simply an enchanting human being, completely human down to the irascibilities and the dislikes that were stronger than reason warranted; a warm man, content to accept the human condition, and very much of his time, yet compromising on no essential point of his beliefs. Once one has read Keats's letters, the knowledge of them cannot but affect the reading of his poems for ever after; so it is with Constable's letters and his painting. Yet it is important to be as unsentimental about Constable's painting as possible; to see it otherwise is to depreciate it.

In his writings he insisted on science almost as much as upon art. 'Painting is a science, and should be pursued as an inquiry into the laws of nature. Why then, may not landscape painting be considered as a branch of natural philosophy, of which pictures are but the experiments?' That rift which now splits what are known as the Two Cultures—of science and of the arts—for him did not exist. Science was the method of art; the purpose of art was poetry. He noted with approval a remark of his friend Jackson, that the whole object and difficulty of art is 'to unite nature with imagination'. His scrutiny of the facts of nature was pertinacious, and as ruthless as it could be in context of the then state of knowledge; what he abhorred above all was the second-hand—in art, especially academic mannerism. He was even against the founding of the National Gallery, because he thought that, with such a collection easily available, 'the manufacturers of pictures (would) then be made the criterion of perfection, and not nature'. The function of the artist should be not to imitate art: all that his predecessors could offer him was experience, in the light of which he could 'get at nature more surely'. Thus he interested himself in the study of colour, its theory and its chemistry; he became almost a professional meteorologist, and after the appearance of Luke Howard's classification of cloud-formations about 1818/20, he became a tireless sketcher of pure cloudscape—'skying', he called it. His finished exhibition pictures most often depend on a whole series of studies of detail; the case-history, noted as scrupulously as any scientific data, on the back of his sketch of *Brighton Beach with Colliers* (p. 80), is typical of his method: '3rd tide receding left the beach wet— Head of Chain Pier Beach Brighton July 19, Evg., 1824'.

In spite of his insistence on working direct from the source, his purpose was never—as the most superficial glance at his work makes abundantly clear—to produce a purely scientific description, a catalogue of category and detail. Art literally imitating nature was for him, besides being impossible, as pointless as art imitating art. When the Diorama, a vast painted panoramic contraption of landscape (it had something in common with the modern Cinerama) was imported for show from France in 1823, Constable found it without the pale of art, 'because its object is deception'. All that Constable aimed to do, scientifically, was to project the most faithful account possible of the *impression* that the scene before him made on his eye. But he knew that the eye is not a machine, to register like a camera; to attempt such a mechanical account would be (as he once accused a colleague of doing) painting nature without the heart in it. The human painter has to select, and he selects according to what excites him most. We know what excited Constable most— a drama, a play and contrast of colour in a lighter key than had been attempted before: a brilliance, a freshness that registers on skin and palate almost as much as on the eyes, and that can be seen even in such an early sketch as the

JOHN CONSTABLE *Cloudscape*

View at Epsom of about 1808 (p. 82); such greens, such yellows, would and did startle his contemporaries ('Take away that nasty green thing!' said a fellow-painter once, in Constable's presence, not realizing that the painting was by him). But the organ that is most excitable in the human make-up is not the eye, but what is loosely known as the heart, and it was with heart and eye that Constable responded. The impression of the eye, in transit to the painter's hand, is affected by the whole nervous and imaginative condition, the state of sensibility, of its owner at the moment he sees. I did not quote the whole of Constable's note on the back of his *Brighton Beach with Colliers;* it goes on: 'My dear Maria's [his wife's] birthday. Your Goddaughter—very lovely Evening—looking Eastward —Cliffs & light of a dark grey effect—background—very white and golden light'. The little painting becomes an exclamation of love, a birthday salute, as light and fresh and aerial in the eye as a lyric by Wordsworth in the ear. The sea's edge curves, taut as a bow from the blue, and the wind comes with it through the immense sky. 'Lovely', he noted on another occasion—'so much so that I could not paint for looking'.

One of the most famous passages in his letters can serve to complement a more wrought-out painting, the *Dedham Mill* (p. 79) of 1820: "The sound of water escaping from mill-dams etc., willows, old rotten planks, slimy posts, and brickwork—I love such things. Shakespeare could make everything poetical; he tells of poor Tom's haunts among 'sheepcotes and mills'. These have always been my delight . . . Painting is with me but another word for feeling, and I associate my 'careless boyhood' with all that lies on the banks of the Stour. These scenes made me a painter, and I am grateful—that is, I had often thought of pictures of them before I ever touched a pencil . . ." Many things lie under the surface of this statement; for one, his abandonment of the 'grand manner'; no classical references, gods or goddesses, inhabit his paintings. Yet his purpose was moral, even as he thought that of painters like Claude had been; he too would have his pictures full (as he felt Gaspar Poussin's were) 'of religious and moral feeling', showing 'how much of his own nature God has implanted in the mind of man'. In this near-religious attitude to landscape of the 'lowest' order he was of course in sympathy with the greatest poets of his age, especially Wordsworth, who answered from such 'a passion and an appetite' to the meanest things in the countryside. And as with Wordsworth, it is Constable's 'lyrics', the swift sketches, that come

JOHN CONSTABLE *View on Hampstead Heath* c. 1823

through with the sharpest urgency and beauty to our eyes today. In his more elaborate, built-up, 'finished' paintings, it often seems as though something had been lost in the process (which was always for Constable very arduous), a vitality for which the greater weight and complexity does not entirely compensate. Yet the 'finished' pictures are what he would wish to be judged by; they are the restatement in modern terms of the grand manner of the past; the sketches were preparatory—'a sketch . . . will not serve more than one state of mind, and will not serve to drink at again and again'. If one accepts that most of his finished pictures do not quite live up to the implications of the sketches then one may feel that though perhaps the greatest painter in England, he did not paint the greatest pictures. On the other hand, he has surely had a more profound influence on the way we see the landscape of England than anyone else; how much more true of Constable himself are the words he applied to Wilson: 'one of the great appointments to show the world the hidden stores and beauties of nature; one of the great men who show to the world what exists in nature but which was not known before his time'. One who enlarged the capacity of our experience.

115

Another point that emerges from his *credo* quoted above, is, for all his new vision, his admitted and modest dependence on, and admiration for, the great painters of the past. 'These scenes . . . I had often thought of pictures of them before I ever touched a pencil'. He saw them in fact, framed in the mind's eye, in a tradition that reaches back through his beloved Gainsborough to his equally beloved Ruysdael, of a painting by whom he wrote: 'The whole is so true, clear and fresh, and as brisk as champagne; a shower has not long passed'. Claude and Poussin he likewise adored, but always in the sense of fellow-experimenters on whose experience he could draw 'to get at nature more surely' on his own. Thus in the later sketch, *A Country Lane*, of about 1826, one can see the hand of a master who has learnt from Gainsborough and from the Dutch, but who is here applying his fully mature technique for his own original purposes. Never before had anyone thus snatched down in paint the sunlight flying through trees and clouds in the moist English air (p. 81).

Constable's immediate influence in England was not great; it was more forceful in France, in part and momentarily on Delacroix himself, and most lastingly on the Barbizon school. In France indeed was working an English-born painter who is in many ways reminiscent of Constable—Bonington, domiciled in France from the age of sixteen until his premature death at twenty-six in 1828. He was a close friend of Delacroix, and in his figure-studies, though they are all on a small scale, he surpasses Delacroix in the force of his rhythm, that almost rivals Rubens. In his landscapes there is that same high key, and the freshness and tang of dew that recalls Constable. In the so-called *Scene in Normandy* (it is more probably located on the plain of St Denis, near Paris), his crisp and brilliant paint is seen at its best, with that characteristic deft placing of the brightly lit accents that looks forward to some of the airy paintings of Boudin (p. 83).

TURNER

Joseph Mallord William Turner was Constable's senior by a year, but outlived him by fourteen. Their careers were as contrasted as their characters. Constable started slowly, almost clumsily, as if groping for the true direction of his genius, and only really began to sight success when he was about forty. Turner swept to the top heights of the profession in his early twenties, borne on by a precocious (and lasting) technical brilliance, a boundless ambition in art, and an almost incredible capacity for work (he left to the nation close on 300 oil paintings that he had not sold, or had bought back, and some 19,000 watercolours). Constable's character is open and clear as a bell, and he wrote his own testament in his letters almost as vividly as in his pictures. The sources of Turner's character are veiled; indeed, as a person, he beetles through the history of English art almost like an animated cartoon character, squat and a little dirty, furtive sometimes as an animal, with solitary hideouts, yet apparently welcome and rewarding company in houses as grand as Petworth; mean as a stone in money-matters, yet generous in his death (in his—partly-frustrated—bequest). Though he fancied himself as a poet he was, verbally, almost incapable of self-expression and communication; but to compensate for that (as well of course as in his painting), he was granted (not that he relished the gift) in his old age a Voice, the resonance of which matches the splendour of his paint: the full eloquence of Ruskin, his passionate apologist and his prophet.

Because of his immense output, and of the variety and the frequently dubious condition in which much of it has survived, it is difficult to be confident that one has arrived at a reliably comprehensive view of his achievement—and Turner was very conscious of his work as a whole— 'What is the good of them but all together?' But it seems clear that his career was basically a constant investigation into light, and a lifelong love affair with paint: the painting of light was his business. Constable too was profoundly concerned with light, and the two in certain oil-sketches can come very close, but for Turner light was the divine principle of the world, the hero-god of his pictures; and it has as such a Shiva-like function, the creator and the destroyer. The material world only exists in the eye when created by light; it was Turner's theme to show how light also dissolved all matter into its own qualities, the colours of the prism.

His pictures are as heroic as any paintings in the classic grand manner, but they are truly superhuman; man and his works are equally subject with the landscape to dissolution by light. Light is triumphant, and one may suspect that for Turner it was almost—if one may put it so—a personification of power. In his most tremendous pictures, it generates and unleashes elemental storm and disaster; it fires the wind that heaves the sea into murder, and the drowning human beings are swept anonymous as shoals of shrimps to death. You do not hear their screams, only the roar of the storm. Even in his visions of calm, inspired so often by Claude whom he admired so much, the sun, dissolving phoenix-wise in its own pyre, dissolves the solid world with it in its incandescence.

The earliest of his paintings reproduced here is one of many evocations of the sea that obsessed him: *The Shipwreck*, of 1805 (p. 85). It was painted at a time when he was still bent on showing his powers in direct rivalry with the masters of the past, and this is an essay on a theme first stated in England by the Van de Veldes, but in terms infinitely more naturalistic, and more violent. The drama of light is not yet the dominant one; as composition it is anchored firmly in the two repeating bright triangles of the sails (although the tilt of these, as if in counterpoint, speaks literally of disaster); through them a strong diagonal thrust comes up and out from the livid light on the horizon on the left, crossed by an equally strong impulse from right to left, the swirling undulation of the trough of the huge white wave that will break in the next second over the wallowing rowing-boat. In the next picture in time—it is of twenty years later, 1835—light proceeds calmly about its business, but transmuting none the less firmly all things into its own terms, until they become dreams or ghosts of substance, holding but tenuously to their physical dimensions and identities under the insidious assault of reflection and refraction; the weight of the black gondola seems less than that of its shadow. The Venice, that Canaletto once painted sharp as diamonds, is drowning, awash with light (p. 86). In the same year, Turner also showed one of his several recordings of the *Burning of the Houses of Parliament* (p. 87). (This happened on the night of 16 October 1834, and Turner, judging by the visual memoranda in a notebook in the British Museum, went out to watch and to record). The scene becomes an almost apocalyptic vision, with the dark huddled mass of spectators swagged hushed across the foreground, powerless and hypnotised. What is left of the world is no more than a reflection of fire; the twin towers of Westminster Abbey

JOSEPH MALLORD WILLIAM TURNER *Chichester Channel* 1829

(in whose ghostly uprights the composition holds together) seem to float in the flames, and the far end of the bridge to disintegrate into them. The painting made a great impression when first shown; although it mystified people, the impact was so undeniable that it was accepted. A critic wrote in *The Spectator:* 'The execution of the picture is curious; to look at it close, it appears a confused mass of daubs and streaks of colour; yet we are told the painter worked at it within a few inches of the canvas for hours together without stepping back to see the effect. Turner seems to paint slovenlily—daubing as one would say; yet what other painter preserves equal clearness of colour? Not that we like this scene-painting manner; we should prefer being able to look at a picture near as well as at a distance; but such a one as this we are content to look at in any way the artist chooses—with all its faults'. It is a remarkable example of Turner's capacity for holding the relation of the parts of an immensely complicated subject clear in his mind right through its long execution to the end: a capacity for co-ordination which is of genius. When it was shown at the British Institution, it arrived, according to a fellow-contributor, in a state 'like chaos before creation'. For three hours before the show opened, Turner worked on it, and when he had done, it stood stable and ordered as architecture; in that final modulation, done mostly with the palette knife, he did no more than 'tune' the colour and place the accents, and the picture cohered. When he had finished, 'with his face still turned to the wall, and at the same distance to it, went sidling

119

off, without speaking a word to anyone . . . All looked with a wondering smile, and Maclise remarked, 'There, that's masterly; he does not stop to look at his work; he *knows* it is done, and he is off'.

But a picture shown seven years later, *The Snowstorm* of 1842 (p. 88), which now seems one of his most prophetic and original paintings, was not so warmly greeted. Here he had gone a bit too far ahead of his time for his generation to be able to accept his experiment, let alone understand and be fired by it. It is sometimes said to be unfinished, but Turner alone was ever competent to decide that point. He himself was uncertain about it; his account of its genesis is almost incredible, when you realize that Turner was sixty-seven when it happened. The full title was *Snow Storm— Steam-boat off a harbour's mouth making signals in shallow water and going by the lead,* and Turner himself was out there, on the Admiralty steam packet *Ariel,* off Harwich in a great storm in January 1842: 'I got the sailors to lash me to the mast to observe it; I was lashed for four hours and I did not expect to escape, but I felt bound to record it if I did. But no one had any business to like it'. The critics agreed, but Turner was annoyed by the scale of their scorn; it was called 'a fantastic puzzle' and generally lampooned; its comparison with a 'mass of soapsuds and whitewash' particularly vexed its author: 'I wonder what they think the sea's like? I wish they'd been in it'.

'Pictures of nothing and very like it', said a contemporary. *The Snow-storm,* though even to modern eyes not immediately obvious to read, is not about nothing, and it is very highly organised. It might perhaps be called an attempt to paint nowhere—the loss of all points of reference in a blizzard at sea when the only constant left is the swirling lash of snow and water and smoke. It is also an attempt to convey the material power, the blind, shoving weight, of the flurries of snow, spray and wave; further, it is a curiously personal statement of triumph, of sheer survival. The dynamic centre that spins the picture is the dark wheel of the paddle-boat, that seems to churn the world outward from itself into centrifugal paroxysm, and it is not, here, the elements that converge destructively on the human ship.

The vision called *Bellinzona from the South* (p. 89) is a page from one of Turner's sketch books, probably relating to a trip up the Rhine, and is moving closer to the abstract than *The Snow-Storm;* it is very far from the accurate, topographical kind of drawing on which Turner had served his apprenticeship. The 'story' is about a vision of colour, luminous drifts of

120

JOSEPH MALLORD WILLIAM TURNER *Peace: Burial (of Wilkie) at Sea*
1841-2

colour; across and through these, the light outlines that spell towers, castles and rock, run frail as lace, insubstantial. In such drawings, the colour dropped like shining veils across the white background, the degree of dependence of Turner's oil technique on such watercolour exercises is indicated. There are thousands of them, and in the latter stages they become often purely abstract memoranda of the patterns of depth that contrasting and complementing patches of colour create on the flat white

121

paper. His pursuit of colour was largely empirical, but based also on a study of theory. His annotated copy of the English translation (1840) of Goethe's *Farbenlehre*, for example, still exists, and he even titled a picture at the Academy in 1843 as *Light and Colour (Goethe's Theory)*; Goethe, amongst other things, associated particular colours with particular states of mind, a counterpoint that can be followed in some of Turner's compositions.

Turner's reflection of the sympathies of his time scarcely needs stressing; he was the most complete expounder in visual terms of the literary and emotional themes of Romanticism—the romance of Walter Scott, the cult of nature particularly in its extreme gestures of soaring mountain, of shoreless sea (the archetypal romantic image perhaps) and incandescent sky; his castles are battlemented, haunted and often ruinous. But also, in so many ways, he points forward out of his time. In his investigation of colour he anticipates in some degree the practice of the Impressionists; in some late works, when colour seems to become arbitrary in the sense that it is independent of the forms it no longer describes, he anticipates, sometimes the Fauves and more often certain of the twentieth century Expressionists and the purely abstract painters—and still, in the 'fifties and 'sixties of this century, his relevance is acute. Already in 1799, he told Farington that he had no 'settled process', but 'drove the colours about till he had expressed the Idea in his mind'—a statement which, isolated, and given only the slightest of twists, could have been made by an Action painter. In fact, in certain later pictures of his, all attempt at shaping the composition in any way hitherto understood, has vanished, and it depends on the tensions and gestures of the paint's run, slash, and flood of colour alone.

BLAKE

Earlier, I quoted William Blake on the gospel of 'particularizing', and the heresy of 'generalizing'. Yet, it is obvious that he generalized in his visual work to a degree that his contempories had no hesitation in qualifying as 'like mad'. But if we look into Blake's vocation more closely, the meaning of what he called 'particularizing' becomes clearer. A firm anti-governmental radicalism influenced all that he did; not least amongst his hatreds was 'official' art; this certainly sharpened his odium of Reynolds, President of the Academy, and of naturalistic landscape. His whole life was spent in relative poverty and obscurity, and he was never the centre of any sort of fashionable enclave. Looking back, he wrote that 'Inspiration and Vision' was from his youth 'and now is, and I hope will always remain, my element, my eternal dwelling place'. He was the personal visionary, the individualist; the only external authority that he was prepared to admit was that of his own inspiration. To particularize, for Blake, meant simply to do what your private, particular, vision told you to do; he looked within rather than without, and depicted this inner vision. The human make-up being what it is, however, the vision could not but embody itself in a shape strongly influenced by what his eye had absorbed, and that from other art rather than from nature. He drew on Michelangelo (as did Reynolds and Lawrence), and also on ancient Greek sculpture and English gothic forms. In his exhibition catalogue of 1809, he promised 'Real art, as it was left us by Raphael and Albrecht Dürer, and Julio Romano, stripped from the ignorances of Rubens and Rembrandt, Titian and Correggio, by William Blake'. But, abandoning scientific perspective, and any attempt at naturalistic illusion, he used his eclectic anatomy of art in a way that was at once decorative, symbolic, and essentially spiritual. To understand the origins of his art, it must be remembered that he was trained as an engraver, was one of the greatest lyric poets ever to use the English language, and was also the profuse prophet of a new and still imperfectly understood mythology. His painting is normally watercolour (or a variation of it; he was a vigorous technical experimenter), and, rather than watercolour, more strictly coloured drawing; it has always something of the book illustration about it, and his experiments in book production were remarkable and original, an attempt to fuse image and word, as in the colour-printed and hand-tinted *Prophetic Books*. The essential surge and exhilaration of his drawing come from what he called the 'flaming line', and his art—which escapes from European canons of what is art as does late Elizabethan painting (both are very difficult to export to foreign taste)—is the supreme example of what is generally held (though how Reynolds or Turner are accommodated to this opinion it is hard to see) to be a specific, essential quality of the English visual character—the emphasis on line. Yet perhaps his paintings are better described as poems visualized, than as illustrations; dream a dream, and lasso it with a line. If their literal interpretation is often obscure (when dependent on his own obscure religious mythology), their intense vitality and exhilaration, and their spiritual grandeur, have a naked and direct impact, and do not fail his inspiration. The *Adam and Eve and the Archangel Raphael* (p. 84) was in fact designed as illustration (one of a series for *Paradise Lost* made in 1808) and is entirely lucid. Adam, Eve, echo Michelangelo and Greek sculpture; the 'scene' is framed as in an engraved border, by a schematized foliage as crisp and vital as English 'stiff-leaf' carving from Southwell. Raphael's wings burn ceaselessly in a perfect ogee, which is also the hallucinatory shape of a candleflame. Such is the intensity of this hybrid, and its perfect co-ordination, that it lives on its own life, although if described in terms of normal iconography and style analysis, it could only sound slightly absurd. Mysterious, luminous, and haunting as an illuminated initial from a mediaeval manuscript, it is as crisp with enduring vitality as the not dissimilar forms of Fuseli, Blake's contemporary to whom he owed so much, are now flaccid. (To dismiss Fuseli so briefly is unjust; yet, though his work was of immense and wide influence, he remains as it were an *eminence grise* behind the scenes; only in his drawings do his great intellectual capacity and the fervour of his vision seem to be matched by his practice).

Blake's attitude to art was symptomatic; once all authority is cast off, and the standards that remain appear to be entirely intuitive and subjective, it becomes much harder for the average spectator to understand his work. For the genius, as Blake was, this does not in the end matter, as the mysterious vitality that genius inspires into its works endures, and will continue to get its response. But for the average artist who relies upon inspiration but does not possess it, this attitude means that his work will be still-born, not even enjoyable as an exercise in a tradition. At all levels except the highest, communication between artist and spectator will tend

WILLIAM BLAKE *Pity* c. 1795

to break down. Blake's contemporaries, quite naturally, said that Blake
was mad, even as Picasso is still held today to be mad by certain circles.
Blake was not mad; he was an explorer, a crotchety English eccentric,
and a genius; he had visions and set them out for all to see. On 12 August
1827, he 'sang loudly and with true ecstatic energy, and seemed so happy
that he had finished his course', and at 6 that evening he died. His song
continues, and so do his pictures, even if they rarely capture so fully the
complete, sharp purity of the lyrics.

The spiritual, almost revivalist fervour of Blake for art found its
disciples towards the close of his life amongst a band of enthusiastic very
young men who had come to know him, and their careers illustrate
something of the glories and perils of the visionary's way of art. The peril
is—as Blake himself never quite did—to lose the vision. This group,
notably George Richmond, John Linnell (rather older than the others),
and especially Samuel Palmer, were responsible for a brief flowering of

pastoral art, and are associated with the name of the village of Shoreham in Kent. It lasted less than ten years and then they went their ways: Richmond to become a polished rather hygienic taker of portrait-likenesses ('The truth? Yes, but the truth lovingly told'); Linnell to become a prosperous, though slightly eccentric, and lush painter of rustic sweeps of Surrey; Palmer to become an able Victorian watercolourist in the main-stream tradition. Yet Palmer's early drawings and watercolours stand alone in English art; though he was certainly influenced by Blake's woodcuts for the Pastorals of Virgil ('visions of little dells, and nooks, and corners of Paradise; models of the exquisitest pitch of intense poetry') his description of them fits many of his own pictures more aptly than Blake's; from the latter he inherited rather a quality of enthusiasm than anything else. He was in line with the then wide-spreading passion of Christian nature mysticism, and moved especially by the pastoral poems of Milton. His paintings are often drawn out of the night or the dusk, heavy with silence and the slow swell of ripening; they are perhaps the densest pictures in English art, their design as close-woven, as organic as the cell-structure of a living organism. The sun sets on them, only for a huge moon to reveal with shadow what the sun hid, a more primaeval, essential shape for the world. They are also the most truly blessed pictures painted in England since the Renaissance, landscapes of contemplation and of adoration.

The peace, this sense of unity and of serenity, abides in the *Cornfield by Moonlight* of about 1830 (p. 90). Six or seven years later, the intensity has failed, the vision faded, and Palmer has become an 'ordinary' painter. His *View at Tivoli* of about 1839 (p. 91), is a professional, able sketch by an English artist on his Italian tour, but the organic coherence has gone for ever; there is even some confusion of organization as the eye travels from foreground to background (one need only glance for comparison at Turner's *Bellinzona from the South* to see where Palmer's view falls to prose). There are hundreds of Victorian watercolours of this kind, and of this agreeable, able but uninspiring level.

VICTORIAN PAINTING

Writing nearly forty years ago, Roger Fry could annihilate, apparently with almost complete justification, the whole of Victorian painting—"the terrible descent in Victorianism" from the heights of achievement of the first forty years of the nineteenth century, from Constable, Turner and Blake. We have now a longer perspective over the period, and, while Fry's contention that it can show no peaks to match those of the preceding age is still clearly uncontestable, we can see that it does own very respectable heights, and that the upper level of the general plateau is by no means so drear as it seemed.

By the eighteen thirties, the Royal Academy had achieved much of its purpose for the arts, at least in a social sense; art had become entirely respectable, and so had the artist. The section of the public (enlargening at tremendous pace in the booming prosperity of industrial and imperial England) that was well enough to do to be able to buy paintings, did buy them and did love them, in their fashion; the aristocratic patrons are matched or surpassed by the new millionaires emerging from the bourgeoisie, like Vernon who had made a corner in horsecoping for the army in the Napoleonic Wars, or Sheepshanks, from a Yorkshire industrialist family. Art was a flourishing concern, with a solid and efficient organization, the Academy its Stock Exchange. The trouble lay in what this concern was concerned about, and above all the manner of its concern. The ends—truths through experiments—tend to be lost from sight in the profusion of the means. There is not so much the attempt to reveal, lay bare a fresh emotion, as to copy an accepted expression of an emotion. Thus in painting in the grand manner, which flourished with commissions in the Houses of Parliament and elsewhere, the gestures are painted, but the life-force that should impel the gestures evaporates. In other kinds of painting, there is a tendency to take an immediately recognizable likeness of a subject already known to be a reliable stimulus to a certain emotion; thus a painting of a picturesque grouping of trees and water, or of characters in period costume, or of rustics in a farmyard, should arouse the same response in the spectator as the sight of the actual objects themselves. But that, as Constable knew, is not the end of art; it is deception. Yet on the other hand deception offers its own pleasures, and these are none the less real for being of a far less exalted order. Roger

127

Fry's strictures imply that it is a sin to indulge in them; it would seem, rather, pretentious not to indulge in such innocent pleasures as long as they retain their savour and one knows what they are.

It may be best, in attempting to indicate some way through the immense profusion of Victorian painting, to select some of the subjects that most obsessed painters and public alike. Portraiture—in spite of the arrival of photography—continued perennial. Sir David Wilkie, who in his earlier manner had painted some brilliant small-scale portraits, later attempted the grand romantic scale, with formidable success on some occasions, but he died before he had fulfilled his promise. William Etty too painted some portraits of a striking shining ripeness, but is best known for his many studies of the nude which sometimes retain some feeling of intimacy. The romantic overtones of Lawrence's manner gradually evaporated as the Victorian presentation portrait came into its own—formal effigies, state-portraits, often curiously close in aloofness of temper to Elizabethan portraits—to adorn board-rooms, town-halls and public institutions. The most successful Victorian portraits are those painted without public exhibition in mind, private portraits of friends or relatives. The outstanding 'public' painter was George Frederick Watts, whose later portraits are inspired, on occasion successfully, by a high moral purpose—to paint the moral grandeur of his sitters' characters. But they are very far from the direct painting of the very youthful self-portrait reproduced here, which has a verve that Watts later lost entirely; this might be a likeness of Shelley (p. 92).

Genre painting was perhaps the great success of the century. The taste came in to respectability at the close of the eighteenth century, with a serious interest in seventeenth century Dutch and Flemish painting. The finest of the British exponents was the young Wilkie—known as the English Teniers—with pictures of village life and festival which, although they may be somewhat shallow in form, have an irresistible boisterousness and verve. The taste widened to include scenes from mediaeval life and battle (à la Walter Scott); from literature—*The Vicar of Wakefield, Gil Blas*, and then Dickens visualized by Dickens' favourite painter, W. P. Frith; from the stage and from poetry. The gaiety and pathos of animal life were especial favourites, and Landseer could render the last moments of a stag in pictorial language (often of great technical brilliance) of the grand manner. In the 'fifties attention turned too to scenes from contemporary life, not only in the hands of the Pre-Raphaelite artists, but in

WILLIAM ETTY *Venus and Cupid* c. 1840–5 129

SIR DAVID WILKIE *The Ratcatchers* 1811

those of Frith and others, and in the 'seventies the more radical of such painters, like Frank Holl, produced paintings of a genuine social realism in their studies of slum life—studies that had great influence on Van Gogh. For urban patrons, throughout the period, rural idylls of cows, picturesque trees and country scenes, retained an inexhaustible attraction.

Much of all this, painted in sound academic technique, still retains considerable charm for most people. Frith's *Derby Day* is at the least brilliant journalism, even if it conveys perhaps an overall impression of charade rather than of pullulating crowd. Such work is after all that of able, intelligent professionals, serious in their work even if seriousness seems too often to have become confused with earnestness. Nor is the flash of a more intense, exploratory creativeness altogether lacking. In the 'fifties one such was manifest in the work of the Pre-Raphaelites and those who shared their fervour. The original aims of the Pre-Raphaelite Brotherhood were to have genuine ideas and to express them, and to study directly from nature. The impulse that fired them was perhaps primarily a moral rather than an artistic one (if the two are separable), but above all theirs was the earnest, ardent (and, alas! perishable) enthusiasm of youth; the most important of them were Millais, Holman Hunt, and Rossetti (to whose Italian revolutionary fervour the idea of a secret brotherhood was due). Whatever the exact effect of the style of the predecessors of Raphael on their own style may have been, they certainly achieved a greater clarity and vividness than any of their contemporaries; they emphasized exact detail, while at the same time carrying over something of the sharpness, the physical weight of that detail into the symbolism of their stories. Arthur Hughes (not an original Brother) has this quality in his *Tryst* (p. 94); it is in mood with the poetry of Keats and of Tennyson, and sighs of one of the essential themes of Victorian romance —unrequited, unrequitable love—expressed here with remarkable restraint and subtle tenderness of expression; the overtones of lily and garden, with their religious associations, yet so precisely and 'realistically' studied, invest the painting with a kind of brooding poignancy. Ford Madox Brown, a close friend of the Pre-Raphaelite movement, applied its principles with ruthless tenacity in such problem pieces as his famous *Work*, conceived as a social critique and wrought out in detail that stifles the whole by excess; he achieved nevertheless a remarkable unity of vision in his rare landscapes. The tiny *Carrying Corn* (p. 93) in the Tate seems projected on to the canvas by the low sun behind you that lances

131

the long shadows into it; across the broad planes of colour, sharp-edged as on a lantern slide, the detail ripples in the calm of a harvest evening, the pale moon already in the clear sky; a condensation of calm and of achievement.

The fire went out of the Pre-Raphaelites and their sympathisers, most of them, within a decade. The 'fifties saw too the climax of Landseer's reputation, and the 'sixties the budding of Victorian ideal painting that flowered on through the 'seventies in a moral earnestness that never found (as it did in France for example with Courbet and even Millet) its true pictorial expression. Against it, in the 'seventies, Whistler hurled thunderbolts in paint and even more in words (1877 was the date of Ruskin's invective against the 'coxcomb' who charged 200 guineas for 'flinging a pot of paint in the public's face', which provoked Whistler's famous libel action against him). And Whistler brings us in sight of, and all but in contact with, the stirrings of the new art in France—Impressionism, leading to Post-Impressionism and the revolution of Cézanne, that was to disrupt the Renaissance conception of art. Whistler, trained in France, was revolutionary enough in England, although his famous impressions of London dusks and fogs have no real relationship to the scientific theories of light put into practize by the Impressionists. Yet his use of almost flat, silhouette pattern (influenced by the Japanese) was new, and shocking, but still more significant was his attitude to the subject matter of his art. He refused to call his beautiful meditation on his mother a portrait; the subject of the picture, he said, might be of interest to him, but not to anyone else; the true subject was the form, the design, the colour—so he called it '*Arrangement in Grey and Black*' (p. 95). Though this was an over-statement (for most people now, a great part of this painting's charm derives from the contrast of the austere design with the typically Victorian sweetness of characterization of the old lady), it points forward to the ever-growing interest in purely formal values that has since turned picture-making so far away from 'nature' (as it had previously been understood) in the last hundred years. Another way in which this new attitude would develop is shown in the work of Walter Greaves, the son of a London boatman who worked for Whistler for a time; whether or not the *Boat Race Day* (p. 96) was painted pre-Whistler (in 1862, when Greaves was sixteen) as the artist claimed, it achieves a curious combination of sophistication and primitive directness; it could have been painted any time in the last sixty years.

132

SIR JOHN EVERETT MILLAIS Detail, from *The Blind Girl* 1854–6

This short introduction has been confined to painting between two great artistic revolutions—that of the Renaissance and that of Impressionism and Post-Impressionism. The course of English painting throughout, in relation to the main European stream, was capricious, and too often much of it provincial in the bad sense, superficially imitative. Yet against that stand the achievements of Hogarth, of Reynolds, of Gainsborough and Lawrence, and of Constable, all masters in a European context; and the native Englishman may well find English painting most exciting, most mysteriously disturbing, when it is at its most boldly eccentric, most provincial, as with the late Elizabethans, with Blake, with Turner. Then it thrusts away in explorations the outcomes of which are scarcely explicable in terms of European painting, but which live in their own splendid validity.

133

FOR FURTHER READING

Many general studies of English painting exist, which cover the subject in greater detail than this short introduction can do. The best recent study is E. K. Waterhouse, *Painting in Britain*, 1530–1790 (Pelican, 1953; the companion volume on the later period is in preparation by Jonathan Mayne). Also indispensable are the volumes, now appearing, of the *Oxford History of English Art*, and those of the *Period Guides* (edited by R. Edwards & L. G. G. Ramsey; published by the Connoisseur, 1956–).

Other recommended works include:

BAKER, C. H. Collins and Constable, W. G. *British Painting*, 1933.

BINYON, L. *English Watercolours*, 1933.

EDWARDS, R. *Early Conversation Pieces*, 1954.

KLINGENDER, F. D. *Art and the Industrial Revolution*, 1947.

REDGRAVE, R. & S. *A Century of British Painters*, 1866 (ed. by R. Todd, 1947).

REYNOLDS, G. *British Portrait Miniaturists*, 1952.

REYNOLDS, G. *Painters of the Victorian Scene*, 1953.

SITWELL, S. *Conversation Pieces*, 1936.

STEEGMAN, J. *The Artist and the Country House*, 1949.

TAYLOR, B. *Animal Painting in England*, 1955.

Works on individual artists are indicated in the Biographical Index.

BIOGRAPHICAL INDEX

COZENS, Alexander. *1717(?)–1786*

Born in Russia. Studied in Rome, and became a fashionable drawing-master in London; taught at Eton. Father of John Robert Cozens (1752–99), Beckford's chosen watercolourist, and precursor of Girtin. See A. P. Oppé, *Alexander and John Robert Cozens*, 1952.
Illustration page 103

DOBSON, William. *1610–1646* 18

Born in London, and studied probably under Cleyn. Worked in Oxford, painting the besieged Cavaliers, c. 1642–46. See O. Millar & M. Whinney, *English Art 1625–1714* (Oxford History of Art, VIII), 1957.
Illustration page 51

ETTY, William. *1787–1849* 129

Born at York; was a printer's apprentice at Hull before entering R.A. schools in 1807; worked under Lawrence; became A.R.A., 1824, and R.A., 1828. Lived a modest and retired life, devoted to his art. See D. Farr, *William Etty*, 1958.
Illustration page 128

EWORTH, Hans. Working c. *1540–1574* 16

A Flemish painter from Antwerp, believed to be identical with one Hans Eworth (all his paintings are signed *HE*, but his identity is very elusive); working in England, mainly on portraits, from about 1544. See E. K. Waterhouse, in *Painting in Britain 1530–1790*, 1953.
Illustration page 49

FRITH, William Powell. *1819–1909* 131

Born in Yorkshire, studied in London at Sass's school and at the R.A. schools; painted portraits and subject pictures, and later, topical genre scenes. Wrote a very successful *Autobiography*. Became A.R.A. in 1845; R.A. 1853.
Frontispiece illustration

GAINSBOROUGH, Thomas. *1727–1788* 36 seq., 98

Son of a crêpe-maker at Sudbury, worked under Gravelot in London before 1745, and was later influenced by Hayman; in the 'fifties painted mainly portraits at Ipswich, and moved in 1759 to Bath; exhibited at the R.A. but not after a quarrel in 1784.

Moved in 1774 to London. For his living he depended always on portraits, but his chief love was for landscape. See W. T. Whitley, *Thomas Gainsborough*, 1915; Ellis Waterhouse, *Gainsborough*, 1958.
Illustrations pages 37, 61–4, 99

GILLRAY, James. *1757–1815* 104

Political caricaturist of the Napoleonic wars; went mad in 1811, and never recovered. See F. D. Klingender, *Hogarth and English Caricature*, 1944.
Illustration page 105

GIRTIN, Thomas. *1775–1802* 105

Born at Southwark, and trained as topographical draughtsman under Dayes; toured British Isles and visited France; knew Turner and had some influence on his early work. See T. Girtin & D. Loshak, *The Art of Thomas Girtin*, 1954.
Illustration page 75

GREAVES, Walter. *1846–1931* 132

Born in Chelsea and studied under Whistler; became generally known only with an exhibition in 1911.
Illustration page 96

HILLIARD, Nicholas. *1547(?)–1619* 16

Son of a Devonshire goldsmith, and trained as a jeweller; visited France c. 1578, became court-miniaturist to Elizabeth, and engraved the Great Seal. Known to have painted also life-size, but no examples are known; his work declines after c. 1605. See J. Pope-Hennessy, *A Lecture on N. Hilliard*, 1949.
Illustration page 50

HOGARTH, William. *1697–1764* 23

An insatiable Londoner, he trained as an engraver; between 1728 and 1732 began painting conversation and theatre pieces; his first comic series is of 1731. Visited France in 1743 and 1748 but was not impressed. Author of the *Line of Beauty*, 1753; appointed Serjeant Painter in 1757; his last years were clouded by quarrels with former friends, Wilkes and Churchill. He was closely allied to the literary talent of his time, particularly that of Henry Fielding. See R. B. Beckett, *Hogarth*, 1949 (the most reliable list; there is an enormous literature on Hogarth).

Illustrations pages 24, 27, 29, 54–7

HOLBEIN, Hans (the younger). *1497–1543*   14

German, born in Augsburg; went to Basle, 1514. The friend of Erasmus and Thomas More. In England 1526–28, and from 1531 till his death of the plague in London. Profoundly influenced by North Italian painting. In England he designed for engravers and metalworkers, and above all painted portraits. See P. Ganz, *The Paintings of Hans Holbein*, 1950

Illustrations pages 12, 15

HUGHES, Arthur. *1830–1915*   131

Born in London, and studied under Alfred Stevens and at the Royal Academy Schools; associated with the Pre-Raphaelites after 1850 but his career after c. 1865 is almost entirely obscure. See in R. Ironside & J. Gere, *Pre-Raphaelite Painters*, 1948.

Illustration page 94

KNELLER, Sir Godfrey. *1649(?)–1723*   21

German-born, studied in Holland and in Italy; came to England c. 1674, and became the most fashionable portrait-painter until his death. His output was enormous, aided by a large studio; knighted 1692, and made a baronet 1715. See in M. Whinney & O. Millar, *English Art 1625–1714*, (Oxford History of Art, VIII), 1957.

Illustration page 20

LAWRENCE, Sir Thomas. *1769–1830*   107

Born in Bristol, became a boy-prodigy, taking portraits in pastel from the age of twelve onwards. Came to London 1786 and was already an A.R.A. in 1791; succeeded Reynolds as Painter to the King in 1792, and elected R.A. 1794; knighted 1815, and President of the Academy from 1820; visited Europe 1818–20 and painted the leaders of the Allies. He was a tremendous worker, but his success dogged always by complete financial incompetence. See

D. Goldring, *Regency Portrait Painter*, 1951; K. Garlick, *Sir Thomas Lawrence*, 1954.
Illustrations pages 76–7, 110

LELY, Sir Peter. *1618–1680*   18

Born in Holland and trained under de Grebber; came to England
c. 1643, and became painter to the Parliamentarians and then to
the Restoration Court; the most fashionable portraitist of his time;
knighted 1680. See in M. Whinney & O. Millar, *English Art 1625–
1714* (Oxford History of English Art, VIII), 1957.
Illustration page 52

MADOX BROWN, Ford. *1821–1893*   131

Born Calais, trained in Bruges and Antwerp (under Wappers). In
London associated with the Pre-Raphaelites (Rossetti was his
pupil). See in R. Ironside & J. Gere, *Pre-Raphaelite Painters*, 1948;
F. M. Hueffer, *Ford Madox Brown*, 1896.
Illustration page 93

MILLAIS, Sir John Everett. *1829–1896*   131

Born Southampton; entered R. A. Schools in 1840. Co-founder of
Pre-Raphaelite Brotherhood, and became A.R.A. in 1853; after
1860, his style altered radically and he became a fashionable
portrait-painter. R.A. 1863, and President from 1896; created a
baronet in 1885. See J. G. Millais, *Life and Letters of Sir J. E. Millais*,
1899: R. Ironside & J. Gere, *Pre-Raphaelite Painters*, 1948.
Illustration page 133

PALMER, Samuel. *1805–1881*   126

Born in London; the decisive factor was his meeting with Blake
in 1824. Lived at Shoreham for about seven years from about
1827, and there produced his most remarkable paintings. In 1838
he married Linnell's daughter, and settled to a career as a rather
conventional watercolourist, and illustrator of Milton. See
G. Grigson, *Samuel Palmer*, 1947.
Illustrations pages 90–1

RAEBURN, Sir Henry. *1756–1823*   107

Born in Edinburgh, he became the principal Scottish portrait
painter, largely self-taught; a brief Italian visit, 1785–7, did not

affect him much. A.R.A. 1812; R.A., 1815; he was knighted in 1822. See Sir W. Armstrong, *Raeburn*, 1901.
Illustration page 70

RAMSAY, Allan. *1713–1784*   46

Born in Edinburgh, much influenced by travels in Italy in 1736–8; worked with Imperiali and Solimena. Settled in London in 1739, and became very successful. Painted little after 1769. See A. Smart, *The Life and Art of Allan Ramsay*, 1952.
Illustration page 65

REYNOLDS, Sir Joshua. *1723–1792*   30 seq., 45

Born at Plympton Earls, Devonshire, apprenticed to Thomas Hudson in London when seventeen years old; practised on his own from 1743 till 1749, when he left for Italy and spent four years there making intensive studies. On his return he established himself as leading painter in a new style. First President of the Royal Academy, 1769, he delivered there his famous *Discourses;* knighted, 1769. Painted little after 1789 owing to failing sight. See E. K. Waterhouse, *Reynolds*, 1941 (with bibliography); there is a good recent biography by Derek Hudson.
Illustrations pages 47, 58–60, 108

ROWLANDSON, Thomas. *1756–1827*   104

Born in London, trained at the R.A. and in Paris; a very prolific producer of watercolours and illustrations, but dissipated his wealth and health. See A. P. Oppé, *Thomas Rowlandson; his Drawings and Watercolours*, 1923.
Illustrations pages 73–4

SCOTT, Samuel. *1702(?)–1772*   31

Born in London(?), friend of Hogarth and Lambert; he began as Marine painter, but after 1745 did mainly views of London. Retired to Ludlow, 1765. See in E. K. Waterhouse, *Painting in Britain 1530–1790*, 1953.
Illustration page 53

STUBBS, George. *1724–1806*   39

Born in Liverpool; was in York c. 1744–52, where he began to study anatomy; paid a brief visit to Italy probably in 1754. From

1758 was engaged on the studies for his *Anatomy of the Horse* (1766); moved to London about 1759, and became A.R.A., 1780, and R.A., 1781. He was always a horse-painter, though he made attempts at grand historical compositions with animals. See B. Taylor, *Animal Painting in England*, 1955.

Illustrations pages 40–2, 69

TOWNE, Francis. *1740–1816*   102

Born in Exeter, and lived there most of his life, working both in oils and watercolour, exhibiting in London. Toured Wales, Italy and Switzerland, and the Lakes. See A. P. Oppé, in *Walpole Society*, vol. VIII, 1920.

Illustration page 72

TURNER, Joseph Mallord William   117

Born in London, son of a Convent Garden barber; trained at the R.A. Schools, and exhibited constantly from 1790 almost till his death. Began as topographical watercolourist and oil-painter; travelled extensively abroad particularly after the Peace in 1815. His early landscapes influenced by Wilson, J. R. Cozens and Claude. Elected A.R.A. 1799; R.A. 1802. In 1826, he set up house in Queen Anne Street, and lived a most secluded life, painting in prodigious quantity, caring little whether his later, revolutionary work pleased the public. He bequeathed his work to the nation. See A. J. Finberg, *Life of J. M. W. Turner*, 1939 (with select bibliography).

Illustrations pages 85–9, 119, 121

VAN DE VELDE, Willem the Elder (*1611–1693*), and his son, Willem the Younger   (*1633–1707*)   21

The father was born at Leiden, Holland, and famous for his grisaille studies of ships; he came to England with his son, in 1673, and both remained here until their deaths. They worked for Charles II, James II and William III. See in E. K. Waterhouse, *Painting in Britain 1530–1790*, 1953.

Illustrations page 22

VAN DYCK, Sir Anthony. *1599–1641*   17

Born in Antwerp, closely associated with and profoundly influenced by Rubens; he was briefly in England 1620-1, but thereafter in Italy and Flanders until he settled here in 1632; he worked especially

for Charles I and his court. For reproductions of his work, see
G. Gluck, *Van Dyck*, 1931 (in German); also L. Cust, *Anthony van
Dyck*, 1900, and, especially for his English period, in M. Whinney
and O. Millar, *English Art 1625–1714*, (Oxford History of English
Art, VIII), 1957.

Illustrations pages 18–19

WATTS, George Frederick. *1817–1904*   129

Born in London, a child prodigy; he won first prize in the Houses
of Parliament competition in 1843, and then visited Italy till 1847.
Made an unsuccessful marriage with Ellen Terry, 1864. Elected
A.R.A. and R.A. in 1867, and became the grand old man of
British portraiture. O.M., 1902. See R. Chapman, *The Laurel and
the Thorn*, 1945 (with bibliography).

Illustration page 92

WHISTLER, James McNeill. *1834–1903*   132

Born at Lowell, Massachusetts, starting as a draughtsman in the
U.S. Coastal Survey; he never returned to America after leaving
for Paris in 1855; knew Courbet, Degas and Fantin-Latour.
Settled in London 1859. The enfant terrible of Victorian Painting.
Pennell's *Life* is still the most important book.

Illustration page 95

WILKIE, Sir David. *1785–1841*   129

Born at Cults, Fife; studied in Edinburgh and at the R.A. Schools;
began by painting genre subjects. Became A.R.A., 1809; R.A.,
1811; Painter in Ordinary to George IV, 1830. His style broadened
after a visit to Italy and Spain, and was not so popular as his early
manner. See in T. S. R. Boase, *English Art 1800–1870*, (Oxford
History of English Art, X) 1959.

Illustration page 130

WILSON, Richard. *1714–1782*   34

Born in Penegoes, Monmouthshire, the son of a clergyman; came
to London, 1729, to study painting and set up practice as portraitist; when in Italy (c. 1750–7) he changed to landscape. A
founder member of the Royal Academy, he never found a widespread popularity. Retired to Wales at the close of his life. See
W. G. Constable, *Richard Wilson*, 1953.

Illustrations pages 35, 66–7

WRIGHT ('of Derby'), Joseph.   *1734–1797*

Born at Derby, to which he returned after 1777. Trained as portraitist under Hudson in London, later specialising in forced light
effects in subject pieces; in Italy 1774–5. Made A.R.A., 1781, but
quarrelled with the Academy soon after. See in E. K. Waterhouse,
Painting in Britain 1530–1790, 1953.
  Illustration page 68

ZOFFANY, Johann.   *1734/5–1810*   18

German, born in Frankfort; he worked in Italy and Germany
before settling in England about 1758, where he worked under
Benjamin Wilson for a time; he was much favoured by George III,
painting conversation pieces and portraits. Worked in India 1783–
90. R.A. 1769. See in E. K. Waterhouse, *Painting in Britain,
1530-1790,* 1953.
  Illustration page 71

*The text is printed in Holland
by Drukkerij Holland N.V.
and the colour plates in Germany
by Carl Schünemann, Bremen*